DELICIOUS FOOD

FOR A

HEALTHY HEART

OVER 120 CHOLESTEROL-FREE, LOW-FAT, QUICK & EASY RECIPES

JOANNE STEPANIAK

BOOK PUBLISHING COMPANY
SUMMERTOWN, TENNESSEE

Cover photograph: Dave Hawkins Photography Inc.
Cover photo styling: Warren Jefferson
Food Styling: Barb Bloomfield
Cover design: Jeanne Kahan
Interior design: Warren C. Jefferson

Published in the United States by:
Book Publishing Company
P.O. Box 99
Summertown, TN 38483
1-888-260-8458

Pictured on the front cover: Portobello Mushroom Steaks, p. 151, Quinoa Primavera, p.148, Tofu Brochettes, p. 138,

Pictured on the back cover: baked potato with Tofu Sour Cream, p.129, and chopped scallions, Spicy Tofu Steaks with Fresh Tomato Sauce, p. 136

Stepaniak, Joanne,
    Delicious food for a healthy heart : over 120 cholesterol-free, low-fat, quick & easy recipes / Joanne Stepaniak.
        p.   cm.
    Includes index.
    ISBN 1-57067-077-3
    1. Heart--Diseases--Diet therapy.   2. Heart--Diseases--Prevention.
3. Low-fat diet Recipes.   4. Low-cholesterol diet Recipes.
I. Title.
    RC684.D5S83   1999
616. 1'20654--dc21   99-29399
                                                            CIP

09 08 07 06 05 03 02   2 3 4 5 6 7 8 9

To Cynthia and Bob Holzapfel
and all the good folks at Book Publishing Company,
and of course to Michael, as always

CONTENTS

Heart Disease and You

Cardiovascular disease, which includes high blood pressure, coronary artery disease, atherosclerosis, and stroke, is the leading cause of death for both men and women in the United States. According to a recent update from the American Heart Association, cardiovascular disease (CVD) claims about as many lives each year as the next seven leading causes of death combined.[1] Once considered a "man's disease," CVD is devastating to women as well, and claims the lives of more females than the next sixteen causes of death combined. In fact, one in two women will eventually die of heart disease or stroke compared to one in twenty-six women who will eventually die of breast cancer. Cardiovascular disease can also affect people in their prime of life. Although the risk of heart disease and stroke continues to rise with age, around one-sixth of people who die from CVD are under age sixty-five. The harsh truth is that about every thirty seconds an American will suffer a heart attack, and almost every minute someone will die from one.

CVD also strikes regardless of race or ethnic origin. African-Americans develop hypertension more severely and at an earlier age than whites and consequently have a greater risk of heart disease. The death rate from cardiovascular disease for African-American men is roughly fifty percent higher than for white men and about sixty-seven percent higher for African-American women than for white women. Cardiovascular disease also leads all other causes of death for people of Hispanic, Asian, and Native American descent in the U.S.

For people who have already had one heart attack, sudden death occurs four to six times the rate of the general population. Cardiovascular disease is frequently a silent killer; many of those who suffer from CVD are unaware they even have the disease. Over half the women and nearly half the men who died suddenly of coronary artery disease had no previous symptoms.

Heart disease affects virtually everyone in North America, directly or indirectly. There is a high probability that you or someone close to you will suffer or die from it. However, from what we already know about heart disease, there is much we can do to avoid or overcome it. In fact, our greatest weapon against heart disease may not lie in drugs or surgery; the solution may be right at the end of our fork.

❦ *Causes of Heart Disease*

Heart disease develops slowly and progressively over several decades of life, sometimes beginning as early as childhood.[2] Its progression is complex, and often there are no specific signs or symptoms until it is too late.

Numerous factors may contribute to the development of heart disease, so it is not always easy to determine specific cause and effect. Nevertheless, extensive clinical and statistical studies have identified several major risk factors that are definitively associated with a significant increase in the risk of coronary artery disease (heart attack). These encompass heredity (including race, sex, and genetic predisposition), age, obesity, sedentary lifestyles, smoking and exposure to tobacco smoke, various other medical conditions and diseases (such as high cholesterol, high blood pressure, and diabetes), and diets high in saturated fat and cholesterol.

Atherosclerosis is one of the most common cardiovascular diseases in the United States. It involves the hardening and narrowing of blood vessels (especially the arteries) from a buildup of fatty deposits called plaques, which are made up of cholesterol, fat, calcium, and other substances. Atherosclerosis affects organs that rely on blood for oxygen and nutrients including the heart, brain, kidneys, and reproductive organs. Plaques can impede the flow of blood and sometimes become so large that they close an artery completely. When this happens to a coronary artery (an artery that supplies blood to the heart), a heart attack occurs. When this happens to an artery that supplies blood to the brain, a stroke occurs.

Because cholesterol cannot dissolve in the blood, it attaches to proteins that transport it around the body. The complete package of cholesterol and protein is called a lipoprotein. There are two types of lipoproteins: low-density lipoprotein (LDL) and high-density lipoprotein (HDL). LDLs (also called "bad" cholesterol) transport cholesterol to various tissue cells in the body, including the walls of blood vessels such as the coronary arteries. Consequently, LDLs raise the risk of heart disease. HDLs, known as "good" cholesterol, carry cholesterol away from the arteries to be broken down and excreted, thereby playing a protective role against heart disease. High LDL levels and low HDL levels are both considered significant risk factors for heart disease. High LDL cholesterol levels combined with other major risk factors, such as high blood pressure, obesity, diabetes, and cigarette smoking, increases the risk even more. The ideal situation is to minimize as many risk factors as possible and maintain low total cholesterol levels with relatively high HDL levels.

❧ *Diet and Heart Health*

Although a person's blood cholesterol level is determined in part by age, sex, and heredity, it is also greatly influenced by diet. Saturated fat, found abundantly in foods of animal origin, raises blood cholesterol levels more than any other dietary component. Dietary cholesterol, which is found only in foods of animal origin, also raises blood cholesterol levels. Contrary to popular belief, even animal products that are very low in fat may still be extremely high in cholesterol. For instance, chicken has about the same cholesterol content as beef.

Trans-fatty acids are formed when vegetable oil is hydrogenated to make it solid and may also raise blood cholesterol levels. These solid vegetable fats are often called "funny fats," because instead of providing nutrients, they make it difficult for natural fatty acids to function properly in the body. Trans-fatty acids are found in most commercial baked goods such as breads, cookies, crackers, and cakes, as well as in margarine and vegetable shortening.

Many studies have shown that vegetarians and vegans (people who eat a totally plant-based diet) have lower blood cholesterol levels than meat eaters. This makes sense because, in addition to consuming no meat, vegetarians on average tend to consume less cholesterol-rich butter, cow's milk, cheese, and eggs, and vegans consume none. One well-publicized study conducted by Dr. Dean Ornish of the University of California, San Francisco, demonstrated that a very low-fat vegetarian diet could not only reduce blood cholesterol levels, it could actually reverse heart disease by reducing the amount of plaque in the arteries.[3] This finding was particularly significant because it was the first time this had been achieved without the use of drugs or surgery.

Dr. Ornish's diet restricts fat to ten percent of calories and allows no animal foods except limited amounts of nonfat dairy products. The program also involves exercise and stress management, which includes daily meditation. In addition to many other benefits, regular physical activity can lower blood pressure. Stress, on the other hand, can drive it up, and over the long run it can take a toll on the heart. Although it may be impossible to eliminate all sources of stress in our lives, it is valuable for both our mental and physical well-being to find ways to manage it. Regular aerobic exercise, even an activity as simple as a brisk walk several times a week, can clear the mind, refresh the spirit, energize the body, reduce blood pressure, and strengthen the heart. It may be that the combined effects of exercise, stress management, and a low-fat vegetarian diet are what have made the Ornish program so successful. Subsequent research by Dr. Ornish also acknowledges the transformative power of love and supportive relationships, and emphasizes the critical role of happiness in healing.

Reduced consumption of cholesterol-laden foods is only one of several reasons why a vegetarian diet may provide the best protection from heart disease. Vegetarian diets are typically lower in fat and animal protein, and vegan diets are completely devoid of animal protein. These nutrients can elevate cholesterol levels and therefore raise the risk of heart disease. However, plant protein, particularly the protein found in soybeans and products made from them (such as tofu, tempeh, and soymilk), has been shown to effectively lower cholesterol levels—sometimes significantly—especially in individuals with very high cholesterol levels.[4]

Vegetarians also consume more fiber. Soluble fiber, found abundantly in legumes (peas, beans, and lentils), oats, and barley, has been shown to reduce cholesterol levels between five and ten percent.[5] For every one percent decrease in cholesterol, there is a two to three percent decrease in the risk of heart disease. Therefore, including foods abundant in soluble fiber as a regular part of the diet can prove to be significant in preventing, controlling, and even reversing heart disease.

The antioxidants found in fruits, vegetables, and whole grains can also protect against heart disease by preventing the oxidation of LDL cholesterol by unstable oxygen molecules called *free radicals*. LDLs must first be oxidized before they can be taken up by arteries and damage the artery walls. Because antioxidants work to prevent this from happening, they are powerful allies in staving off the damaging effects of cholesterol. Vitamin C and vitamin E also appear to be potent antioxidants. These vitamins tend to be more plentiful in the diets of vegetarians than those of meat-eaters.

High levels of iron can act as catalysts for free-radical damage. The type of iron found in meat may be particularly damaging because it is very rapidly and easily absorbed. Conversely, the type of iron found in plant foods has shown no effect on raising the risk of heart disease.[6] The presence of iron in varying amounts may help explain why men and women have different rates of heart disease. Before menopause, women have a much lower risk of heart disease because their bodies naturally eliminate iron during menstruation. After menopause, when this regular elimination no longer occurs, women's mortality rate from heart disease rises to nearly that of men's.[7] In general, the iron levels of vegetarians tend to be lower than those of meat eaters, but are still within the normal range.

Polyunsaturated fat and monounsaturated fat, the two most common fats in plant foods, can help lower blood cholesterol levels, especially when they replace saturated fat in the diet. Certain monounsaturated vegetables oils, such as olive oil (and, to a lesser extent, canola oil), can have a valuable effect on raising HDL cholesterol levels. Foods that are rich in omega-3 fatty acids may also provide protection from cardiovascular disease by reducing triglycerides in the blood (which play a role in heart disease) and by reducing blood pressure and inhibiting the formation of atherosclerotic plaque. Unrefined flaxseed oil is one of the richest sources of omega-3 fatty acids and more effective in promoting health than fish or fish oil capsules. All fish products contain some measure of saturated fat and significant amounts of cholesterol. Shellfish, ounce for ounce, is higher in cholesterol than beef. Additionally, fish fats are easily broken down by light, air and heat, they encourage the production of free radicals, and frequently contain concentrated amounts of environmental toxins. Although experts recommend a reduction in the consumption of all types of dietary fat, unrefined vegetable oils, such as olive oil and flaxseed oil, may, in limited quantities, play a beneficial role in fending off heart disease.

❧ *Keeping Your Heart Happy*

Change can often seem overwhelming, especially when it involves upending lifelong habits. In the long run, however, modifications to diet, outlook, and everyday activities can powerfully and positively impact longevity and transform health more significantly—and with longer lasting results—than drugs or surgery.

In general, there are several broad lifestyle recommendations consistent with current information on heart disease that can be easily incorporated into most people's lives. These suggestions are sensible, sound, and effective, and can be integrated into your daily routine with little effort or expense.

It is common knowledge that the state of our health is intimately connected to the level of joy and hope we have in our lives. Because our outlook, attitude, and approach to life can dramatically affect our physical well-being, the following lifestyle changes will help maintain a happy heart as well as a healthy one:

1. Quit smoking and eliminate exposure to environmental tobacco smoke.

2. Exercise regularly. Incorporate a daily, low-impact aerobic activity such as walking.

3. Minimize stress, hostility, and anger by facing problems directly and realistically. Then seek practical, reasonable solutions.

4. Face the challenges that lie in front of you today instead of dwelling on problems in the past, the distant future, or ones beyond your control.

5. Be creative! Use your talents and skills to make gifts of art, music, food, or clothing for yourself and others to enjoy.

6. Contribute in whatever way you can to make this world a better place for all. Volunteer to help children, adults, or elders in need. Assist at the local animal shelter. Plant a garden. Visit a lonely neighbor. Read a story to a child. The more you give of yourself, the greater will be your rewards.

7. Enjoy the simple, natural pleasures of life that too often are overlooked or taken for granted.

8. Live each day as if it might be your last, and choose to leave a legacy worth remembering.

9. Don't take yourself or anyone else too seriously.

10. Laughter is the most effective medicine. Keep it handy and use it often.

❦ Ten Steps to a Healthier Heart

The first step in determining the health of your heart is to have a complete physical examination including a full blood workup. Discuss the results with your physician or healthcare practitioner to determine the lifestyle changes you should make to improve or maintain your heart's health. Every person is unique, and your exercise regimen and eating plan may need to be tailored to your individual needs.

We are fortunate to live in a society where food is abundant and relatively accessible. Nevertheless, we are taught very little about how to plan a diet that will keep us healthy, strong, and vital throughout our lives. Most of us tend to wait until we are confronted with serious illness before we consider making fundamental modifications to our eating habits. Unfortunately, by that time it is often too late. Once symptoms begin to appear, it is a signal that our health has already drastically deteriorated, and moderate adjustments to our diet may not be aggressive enough to effect the necessary changes.

The time to transform your diet is now. We know that heart disease is an illness of degeneration that takes many years to develop. It is not the consequence of what you ate yesterday; it is the cumulative result of poor dietary habits amassed over a lifetime. If you alter your diet today, your tomorrows are more likely to be filled with promise and life. Because a wholesome diet is a critical component in achieving and maintaining a healthy heart, consider the following guidelines:

1. Eliminate all animal foods from your diet including meat, fish, fowl, eggs, and all dairy products. Remember that all foods of animal origin contain cholesterol, irrespective of their fat content.

2. Center your diet around unrefined, unprocessed plant foods including vegetables, fruits, whole grains, and legumes. Unrefined whole plant foods contain virtually no cholesterol and are rich in beneficial antioxidants, vitamins, minerals, and fiber.

3. Choose organically grown foods. These foods are not only better for the environment and the farmers who grow them, they are free of toxic chemicals that may further compromise your health.

8

4. Include a source of soluble fiber in your daily diet such as beans, peas, lentils, oatmeal, or barley. Soluble fiber reduces blood cholesterol levels and is found only in plant foods.

5. Include soyfoods such as tofu, tempeh, and soymilk regularly in your diet (unless you are allergic to soy). The protein in soyfoods lowers blood cholesterol levels, and unrefined soy products are good sources of omega-3 fatty acids.

6. Omit butter, margarine, shortening, and refined oils of any kind from your diet.

7. Avoid all commercially prepared baked goods and snack products including refined bread, cookies, potato chips, fried tortilla chips, crackers, and cakes.

8. If you have high blood pressure, limit the amount of salt you put in or on foods—including the sodium in canned, processed, or packaged foods—to approximately ¼ teaspoon, or about 500 to 750 milligrams of sodium, per day. In some individuals, sodium intake is linked to high blood pressure.

9. Avoid commercially processed and refined foods because these tend to be high in sodium and fat and low in fiber and essential nutrients.

10. Include moderate amounts of unrefined olive oil and flaxseed oil in your daily diet—about one teaspoon per meal, or about one tablespoon per day—while limiting all other sources of fat including nuts, seeds, olives, avocado, coconut, vegan mayonnaise, and nut and seed butters.

❧ *Changing Your Diet*

Most health practitioners agree that the more extensive and long-lasting beneficial changes a person makes to her or his diet, the more dramatic and sustaining the health benefits for one's heart. To create enduring vitality requires letting go of damaging habits while simultaneously incorporating healthful practices. This necessitates viewing food in a whole new light.

Most people have busy schedules and don't feel they have the time to cook or eat right. And because prepared fast foods are readily accessible, many people just grab the easiest or quickest items they can find without giving much consideration as to whether they are health supporting or harmful. The result is that North Americans eat considerably more unhealthful and potentially damaging foods than foods that are wholesome and nutritious, opening the door to an onslaught of unnecessary diet-related afflictions, such as heart disease.

Processed commodities such as white bread, chips, pastries, and french fries, are staples of the standard Western diet. These, and many other processed foods, are stripped of nutrition and fiber, then artificially "enhanced" with fat, sodium, vitamins, and minerals, which in no way compensate for what has been removed. By the time most foodstuffs get to our table, they are essentially nutritionally bankrupt. And because these foods make up the bulk of most people's diets, there is little room left for truly healthful products.

Fruits, vegetables, whole grains, and legumes are nutritionally rich, whole natural foods. When switching from the typical North American processed-foods diet to a whole-foods diet, one of the first things people discover is that they must actually chew their food. If your jaw and teeth have gotten sluggish from inactivity, whole grains and fresh vegetables are a great way to put them back into action. Digestion begins with chewing, so the more slowly you eat, and the more thoroughly you grind your food, the more easily and completely the nutrients can be assimilated.

When first adopting a total vegetarian (vegan) diet, many people are concerned about how to adapt. It's a challenge to determine where to begin, and learning anew how to eat may feel overwhelming. At first you may decide to incorporate just a few simple modifications and make broader changes gradually. Bear in mind, however, that the sooner you alter your diet for the better, the faster you'll reap dramatic and beneficial results.

Eliminating or drastically reducing all animal products from your diet is essential if you are serious about reducing your risk of heart disease. Remember, only animal-based foods contain heart disease-producing cholesterol, saturated animal fat, and animal protein. They include none of the heart-protecting antioxidants and micronutrients or cancer-fending fiber found in plant foods. Fortunately, there are some absolutely delicious plant-based products you can use in the place of meat and dairy products. You may even become so enamored with them that your old animal-source foods will pale in comparison. Many people who switch to a total vegetarian diet not only reap enormous health benefits, they are ecstatic about the extensive variety of foods available to them. It's not that these foods are off limits to meat eaters; it's just that people who eat meat rarely look beyond what's on the typical North American plate. A wholly plant-based diet compels people to thoroughly peruse the produce aisles and natural food store shelves. This in itself can be a delightful adventure.

Food is more than something to quiet a growling gut or mindlessly consume while performing other activities. Food is what fuels our bodies, builds and sustains our biological systems, keeps us alert and energetic, wards off illness, and helps prevent disease. Just as we wouldn't put sludge in the fuel tank of our car if we wanted it to run efficiently, we shouldn't put junk into our body if we want it to function optimally.

❦ *Breakfast* ❦

Many breakfast-skippers are prone to the mid-morning munchies, a time when quelling hunger pangs by any means can take precedence over more sensible selections. Typically by lunchtime they are ravenous, and it becomes even harder to make rational choices and pass up unwholesome temptations. A nutrient-dense morning meal helps most people put their best foot forward and provides the energy that's needed to keep going throughout the day.

If you are accustomed to cold cereal with cow's milk in the morning, you can substitute an organic, whole grain cereal and top it with either unsweetened fruit juice or a nondairy beverage (such as calcium fortified soymilk, rice milk, oat milk, or nut milk) instead of dairy milk. Add a few raisins, chopped dates or apricots, sliced banana, or fresh seasonal fruit or berries. Hot cooked grain, such as oatmeal or polenta, or "creamed" grain made from finely ground brown rice, barley, wheat, or other grains, makes a delicious and satisfying porridge. Whole grains soaked overnight in a little extra water and cooked or pressure cooked in the morning will be soft, creamy, and digestible. This may also be served with fresh or dried fruit and juice, soymilk, or grain-based milk (such as rice or oat milk).

Bagels, toast, or low-fat, homemade egg- and dairy-free muffins and quick breads made with whole grain flours are other good breakfast choices. Serve them with fruit-sweetened jam or jelly, a low-fat tofu spread, nut butter thinned with applesauce, or fruit butter (such as apple, prune, apricot, or pumpkin).

On leisurely mornings, make whole grain pancakes, French toast, or scrambled tofu. If you prefer a more savory breakfast, heat up some cooked beans (drained and rinsed to remove excess sodium) with a little salsa or barbecue sauce. Add some chopped lettuce, shredded carrot, or other sliced or grated raw vegetables, and roll the mixture up in a whole wheat chapati or tortilla. Leftovers from last night's dinner can be warmed up (some people even like their leftovers served cold), or you can make a sandwich with tofu and lettuce or a bean spread.

Breakfast should never be a chore. If you need to get up a little earlier in order to have time to eat something nourishing, then you might have to make that concession. Make it a point to always have ready-to-eat foods handy for breakfast, so if you don't have time to prepare something more elaborate, you won't be shortchanged.

❦ *Lunch* ❦

There are plenty of pure vegetarian, low-salt, low-fat meals-in-a-cup to choose from at the natural food store and even the supermarket. These make quick, no-brainer lunches for people on the run. You only need to have access to boiling water and lunch can be steaming hot and ready in mere minutes. Canned vegetarian soups and seasoned beans also make great meals if you have access to a microwave oven or stove. Leftovers are always tasty and can be eaten cold or heated up. Vegetable dips and bean spreads are great with raw veggies, such as carrot and celery sticks, radishes, broccoli and cauliflower florets, or bell pepper strips, and pita bread or bagels. Baked potatoes are filling, served plain or topped with ketchup, salsa, or a fat-free vinaigrette. Some fast food and full-service restaurants offer plain baked potatoes, making them a good choice when you must go out to eat on your lunch break.

Salads from home or the restaurant salad bar are great, but watch the dressings and extras. Potato and macaroni salads are almost always made with greasy, high-fat, egg-based mayonnaise, creamy coleslaw is dairy based, jelled dishes are made from animal by-products, sour cream and other creamy dressings are dairy based and high in fat, and oil-based dressings are made from highly refined products and are very rich in fat. Go for the simplest, most unprocessed items, such as plain carrot sticks and other raw vegetables, dark leafy greens instead of iceberg lettuce (for the highest nutritive value), unseasoned beans, applesauce, and diced beets. Bring your own low-fat or fat-free dressing and whole grain bread or rolls (no butter or margarine).

Sandwich ideas include tofu and bean spreads; smoked or seasoned tofu or seitan (a meat substitute made from wheat); salads made with tofu, tempeh, or vegetables; seasoned cooked vegetables; grain pâtés; precooked veggie burgers or tofu hot dogs; and vegetarian luncheon meats. Use whole grain bread, bagels, chapatis, tortillas, or lavosh for your wrapper.

❦ *Dinner* ❦

Most North Americans are used to having meat or another high-protein animal food, such as eggs or dairy products, at the center of their dinner plates. Pure vegetarian meals, on the other hand, open up a new world of opportunity and interest. Although high-protein plant foods, such as tofu or beans, can certainly be headline acts, grains and vegetables can also serve as the featured attraction. Keep in mind that vegetarian meals shouldn't box you in. On the contrary, they open up fresh vistas for creativity and innovation.

This book offers a variety of entrée recipes, including high-protein soy and bean dishes. Beyond these there are potato, pasta, grain-based, and vegetable-centered meals, each offering an endless number of possibilities. Pasta with tomato sauce and a salad on the side is a familiar and popular dish. Baked potatoes topped with a tofu sour cream sauce or broccoli in a nondairy cheese-style sauce are other conventional choices. How about baked beans with a dairy-free coleslaw and egg-free cornbread? Stir-fried vegetables served over rice offers continual variety. Who wouldn't enjoy macaroni noodles topped with steamed vegetables and a low-fat Italian dressing? In warm weather, try a grand tossed salad with baked croutons, strips of smoked tofu, and a creamy nondairy or low-fat dressing. In colder seasons, serve a hot vegetable or bean stew with crusty sourdough bread. You can even present a simple but beautiful plate of steamed or baked seasonal vegetables with a low-fat dipping sauce on the side. If you incorporate an array of dazzling colors and shapes, even the most avowed vegetable avoider will find the meal irresistible.

❦ *Snacks* ❦

Vegetables and fruits are packed with nourishment, micronutrients, and disease-preventing antioxidants. Keep plenty of fresh organic produce on hand for quick between-meal snacks. If you have access to a refrigerator in your office or place of employment, bring washed and cut up vegetables to work with you, and store them along with a low-fat dressing or dip for a handy energy lift. If you travel often by car, tote along a small cooler. Salt-free pretzels, plain (no butter) popcorn, rice cakes, and baked corn chips with salsa also are great when the afternoon munchies strike. Fresh fruit such as apples, bananas, and grapes, and seasonal delights like berries, pineapple, and melon can be washed and prepared in advance so they're ready whenever you want them. Dried fruit, in moderation, can quickly quash a hunger attack. Keep a box of raisins in your desk drawer or a sealed bag of dried fruit such as unsulfered apricots, pineapple rings, figs, or apples. A wedge of seasoned tofu or a slice of fat-free, seitan-based luncheon "meat" on whole grain bread is another option. Unsweetened fruit juices and fortified nondairy milks in aseptic boxes, flavored amasake (a sweet, fermented rice drink), or blended fruit smoothies are light but filling beverages.

It's certainly not necessary for you to snack to get all your nutritional requirements, especially if you are consuming three meals a day that include a variety of whole foods. Snacks can, however, be a great way to incorporate more fruits and vegetables into your diet and boost your overall nutrition. Just make sure that when you snack, the foods you select are wholesome, low-fat, and low-sodium, and aren't consumed too close to regular mealtime.

❦ *High Flavor With Low Fat and Sodium* ❦

Once you explore the world of whole foods, you'll discover new tastes and fresh, exciting flavors. Whole grains have deep, earthy undertones, a hearty chewiness, and a naturally nutty sweetness. Vegetables burst with vitality and crunch, which seduce the palate and send a savory rush over the discriminating tongue. Beans and legumes are beautiful to behold and luxuriously creamy with subtle qualities that are incredibly rich and sensual.

Whole natural foods are complemented by gentle cooking and simple, minimal seasonings applied with a delicate touch. Explore the variety of magnificent, seasonal fresh herbs, dried individual herbs, and herbal blends available at your supermarket or natural food store. Perk up vegetables and salads with a salt-free dried herb mix. A splash of plain or seasoned vinegar or a squirt of fresh-squeezed lemon or lime juice will make flavors really pop. Low-sodium, naturally brewed soy sauce adds a splendid beefy taste to all kinds of foods. Extra-virgin olive oil and organic flaxseed oil are so flavorful that just a teaspoon or two per serving is generally sufficient to enhance any dish.

Of course, salt does draw out the natural flavors in foods that might otherwise taste flat. The key with both salt and fat is to be conscious of how much you are using, not only at each meal but also throughout the day. If you include commercially prepared or refined foods in your diet, it is very easy to quickly exceed your salt and fat limits for the day. According to the Center for Science in the Public Interest, only ten percent of sodium intake comes from the salt shaker; the remaining ninety percent comes from processed foods![8] Therefore, if you are being careful about your sodium intake and have not been advised by your healthcare practitioner to eliminate salt from your diet, you can comfortably add a moderate amount to recipes or, if you prefer, sprinkle a pinch or so over the top of your food. (A pinch is the tiny amount you can easily grasp between your thumb and forefinger.) When you lightly sprinkle salt over your food instead of mixing it in or adding it during cooking, your food will taste saltier even though it will actually contain less salt. This is because the salty taste will flood your palate from the outset before other flavors subdue it.

❧ *Desserts* ❧

Although most people have a sweet tooth, few people regularly appreciate the mellow, refreshing sweetness found naturally in fresh, ripe fruit. Not only is this the most healthful dessert, it is certainly the easiest to prepare. Make fresh fruit your staple dessert. Most fruits are virtually fat-free, low in sodium, high in fiber, succulent, vibrant, nutritious, and delicious.

But what if you want something really decadent once in a while? Many people assert that an infrequent thin sliver of a rich cake or other indulgence is far superior to the cardboard-like, fat-free "healthy desserts" they could have more often. I agree, with a few stipulations. If you are the type of person who can't stop after one slice, then stick with the low-fat options and avoid a temptation that could possibly get out of control. Another problem inherent with the occasional treat is that you are in essence taking one step forward and two steps back. The intense sweetness of desserts made with refined sugars, stripped flours, and hydrogenated fats can be alluring and addictive, and you may not be allowing your taste buds enough time and opportunity to adjust to the more gentle flavors of naturally sweet foods. Nevertheless, I've included a few great recipes for rich-tasting but healthful desserts for people whose sweet tooth still has a tight grip on their palate.

❦ A Word of Encouragement

Changing our diet is a scary proposition because our emotions are so deeply tied to the foods we eat. For the majority of us, our earliest lessons about food were taught by our families, bolstered by what we learned from our ethnic backgrounds and the culture at large. Rarely do individuals select foods based strictly on health concerns. Many factors go into our dietary choices including taste, custom, convenience, cost, and familiarity. Most commonly, we eat out of habit and impulse rather than with forethought and intention.

Our ancestors chose particular foods based on what was accessible. Ethnic and regional cuisines grew out of necessity, not design. Even if you were fortunate to be raised in a household where healthful eating was a top concern, current research has proven the dietary assumptions of the last several decades to be not only erroneous but often quite dangerous.

Don't condemn yourself if you have had poor eating habits. Numerous elements influence our food choices, and it's likely impossible, and certainly pointless, to try to lay blame. What is important is that you have clear and positive options you can choose today. We now know that many people can reclaim their health, even after a lifetime of wreaking havoc on their body through poor diet, harmful habits, and lack of exercise. You are not alone! Many people are taking part in the venture toward health and wholeness. As the saying goes: Every journey begins with the first step. May goodness, grace, health, and peace join you on the pathway to well-being.

Bean Basics

Legumes (beans, peas, and lentils) are packed with great earthy flavors. In addition, they are nutritional powerhouses loaded with cholesterol-reducing soluble fiber, bone-building calcium, and high-quality vegetable protein. Keeping cooked beans on hand will give you a head start toward speedy, healthful meal planning.

Canned beans are widely available, unquestionably convenient, and a great alternative when you don't have the time or inclination to cook beans from scratch. Natural food stores generally carry a good selection of organic canned beans. To reduce sodium, rinse canned beans well before using them. A 15-ounce can contains approximately 1⅔ cups of beans. Recipes calling for 1½ to 1¾ cups of beans will turn out fine, even if you use slightly less or slightly more beans than called for. So feel free to interchange 14-ounce, 15-ounce, and 16-ounce cans of beans in your recipes.

To save time and maintain a good inventory of cooked beans, always cook more than you need. Refrigerate the beans you plan to use, then pack the remainder (with or without their liquid) in freezer-safe storage containers or zippered bags. Label and date the containers, place them in the freezer, and use the beans within three months. Home-cooked beans are significantly more economical than canned beans. Moreover, a wider selection of organic beans is available dried than canned, so cooking beans at home will afford greater variety. Natural food stores and mail order suppliers are the best places to find the freshest and broadest assortment of dried beans.

❦ *Soaking Beans*

For faster, more even cooking and better digestibility, most beans should be soaked before cooking. Exceptions include delicate legumes such as lentils, split peas, and black-eyed peas. Beans like a little time to get used to the water before the heat is turned on. In addition, beans contain indigestible sugars that are not eliminated with cooking. When beans are soaked, however, these sugars are released into the soaking water and are washed away once the beans are drained and rinsed. Effective soaking involves immersing the beans in water until the water permeates the center of each bean. There are three easy methods for soaking beans:

- *Long Soak:* Cover the beans with water, and let sit for 6 to 12 hours. This can be done during the day or overnight. In very hot weather, keep the soaking beans in a cool place or in the refrigerator to prevent them from souring.
- *Short Soak:* Place the beans in a large pot. Add enough water to cover the beans by a couple of inches. Bring to a hard boil, remove from the heat, cover, and let the beans sit for 1 to 2 hours.
- *Rapid Pressure Soak:* Place the beans in a pressure cooker, and bring to a hard boil. Lock the lid in place, and bring up to high pressure. Reduce the heat just enough to maintain high pressure, and cook under pressure for 2 to 5 minutes (2 to 3 minutes for small beans, 3 to 4 minutes for medium beans, and 4 to 5 minutes for large beans). Remove the cooker from the heat, allow the pressure to come down naturally, and let the beans sit with the cover in place for 20 to 60 minutes (20 to 30 minutes for small beans, 30 to 45 minutes for medium beans, and 60 minutes for large beans).

To check if the beans have soaked long enough, remove one or two of them with a slotted spoon and slice them in half with a sharp knife. If the beans look evenly saturated and uniform in color, they are ready to be cooked. If the center is still opaque, more soaking is necessary, or you can simply allow a little extra time for cooking.

❦ *Cooking Beans*

Beans take time or pressure to cook. Simmering beans on the stovetop can be relaxing and enjoyable. The beans will require very little tending, although they may take quite a while to become tender. If you serve beans often, or if time is at a premium, pressure cooking is the speediest and most fuel-efficient method. For hassle-free bean cookery, use one of the newly designed "second generation" pressure cookers fitted with a stationary pressure regulator.

Times for cooking beans will vary greatly depending on the age of the beans and the conditions under which they were stored. Beans stored for long periods may become shriveled or dimpled; however, it is not always easy to judge the age of a bean by its appearance. To be sure your beans are fresh, purchase them in small quantities from reputable merchants whose stock is rapidly turned over, and use the beans within a few months. Beans that are very old occasionally become so dried out and tough that it may be impossible to tenderize them regardless of how long they cook.

Salt and acidic ingredients, such as vinegar, tomato products, lemon juice, and molasses can toughen beans, slow down water absorption, and make it more difficult for the beans to soften properly. If you have problems with this, add salt and acidic ingredients to beans only after thorough cooking.

🍎 *Tips For Simmering Beans*

1. Beans must be completely covered with water or vegetable stock at all times during cooking. Usually 3 cups liquid to 1 cup dried beans is sufficient. Add more boiling water or stock during cooking, if needed, so the beans are always covered with liquid.

2. Bring the soaked beans to a hard boil. Reduce the heat, cover, and simmer gently.

3. Beans often create a lot of foam during cooking. An optional 2 to 3 teaspoons of a mild vegetable oil, such as canola oil or olive oil, per cupful of dried beans may be added to the cooking liquid to help keep foam under control.

🍎 *Times For Simmering Beans*

The following estimated times are for simmering soaked beans on the stovetop. Soaking is not required for lentils, split peas, and black-eyed peas, but you can include this step if you want to hasten the cooking time. Cooking times will need to be extended about 30 to 90 minutes for unsoaked beans, and sometimes even longer depending on the bean. Remember that age and other factors greatly affect the amount of time it takes for beans to soften, so these are broad approximations. Check for tenderness about 20 minutes before the minimum recommended time has elapsed.

Split peas, black-eyed peas, and lentils: 30 minutes to 1 hour

Other beans (adzuki beans, anasazi beans, black beans, brown beans, calypso beans, cranberry beans, flageolets, garbanzo beans [chick-peas], great Northern beans, kidney beans, pink beans, pinto beans, red beans, and white beans): 1 to 2½ hours

Soybeans should not be cooked by simmering, as they do not easily become soft without using a pressure cooker.

🐚 *Tips For Pressure Cooking Beans*

1. Fill the pressure cooker no more than halfway, using at least 2½ to 3 cups liquid for each cup of dried beans. Make sure there is plenty of liquid so the beans remain completely covered during the entire cooking time. Remove any floating bean skins so they won't clog the vent of the cooker.

2. If desired, add 2 to 3 teaspoons of a mild vegetable oil, such as olive oil or canola oil, for each cup of cup dried beans to help control foaming.

3. Bring to a boil. Lock the lid in place, and bring up to high pressure. Reduce the heat just enough to maintain high pressure. Begin timing as soon as high pressure is reached.

4. Except for delicate legumes, such as lentils, split peas, and black-eyed peas, always use natural pressure release instead of a quick-release method, which can produce foaming or sputtering at the vent and cause beans to rupture. To release pressure naturally, remove the cooker from the heat and allow the pressure to drop gradually without assistance. This will take about 10 to 15 minutes. To quick-release pressure, place the cooker in the sink and run cool tap water around the rim of the lid, avoiding the vent area, until the pressure drops completely—or follow the manufacturer's instructions.

5. It is best to slightly undercook beans than risk overcooking them. If the beans are not quite tender after the minimum cooking time has elapsed, cover the pot (but do not lock the lid) and simmer the beans without pressure over low heat until done. If the beans are still quite hard or require significantly longer cooking, return them to high pressure for a few more minutes, and again allow the pressure to fall naturally.

6. Allow the beans to cool in the cooking liquid. Clean the pressure cooker lid, vent, and rubber gasket thoroughly and as soon as possible after cooking.

🐚 *Times For Pressure Cooking Beans*

The following estimated times are for cooking soaked beans under high pressure (15 lbs.) and allow for natural pressure release, which takes an additional 10 to 15 minutes. If you choose to use a quick-release method instead, you will need to add 3 to 4 minutes to the pressure cooking time (except for lentils, split peas, and black-eyed peas, which should always be quick released). If you are using unsoaked beans, times will need to be increased by half or possibly doubled. Always begin timing *after* full pressure has been reached.

Split peas, black-eyed peas, and lentils (unsoaked): 4 to 12 minutes

Small beans (such as adzuki beans and navy beans): 1 to 4 minutes

Medium beans (such as pinto beans, kidney beans, great Northern beans, and black beans): 3 to 8 minutes

Large beans (such as garbanzo beans): 10 to 16 minutes

Soybeans: 35 to 40 minutes

❦ *Bean Buddies*

Beans enjoy the company of vegetables such as onions, celery, and carrots. If you want to add vegetables to stovetop simmered beans, sauté them first in a little olive oil or canola oil, and add them to the nearly cooked beans. Simmer them with the beans for about 30 to 40 minutes. For pressure cooking, the vegetables can be cooked right along with the beans.

Regardless of which method you use, vegetables will enhance the flavor of the beans and create a rich, delicious stock. Depending on the amount of vegetables you add, you will end up with beans with vegetables, vegetables with beans, or stew. Other seasoning options that can be added at the start of cooking include garlic, bay leaves, and kombu. Kombu is a sea vegetable high in minerals and purported to improve the digestibility of beans. It is typically available dried and can be found in most natural food stores. Add a one-inch piece of kombu at the start of cooking. After cooking, the kombu can be removed, or you can chop it and mix it back into the beans for added flavor and nutrition.

14 Days of Menus

The following menu plans will help to get you started. Feel free to adjust them or make substitutions to suit your individual needs. For example, serve plain or instant oatmeal instead of the flavored recipes, or use canned or instant soups instead of homemade. Keep your pantry and freezer stocked with convenience foods such as frozen vegetables, veggie burgers and "hot dogs," canned beans, prepared spaghetti sauce, canned fruit packed in juice, dried fruit, nondairy milk and juice in aseptic packages, canned and instant soups, and low-fat, ready-to-eat cereals. Having these foods on hand will make it easier to stick to a healthful diet. Snacks are optional and may be eaten at whatever time you desire. Page numbers are listed for recipes that are in this book.

❦ *Day One* ❦

Breakfast

Orange-Apricot Oatmeal, p. 32; 2 slices whole wheat toast with 2 teaspoons almond butter; 6 ounces apple juice; 1 cup fortified nondairy milk

Lunch

½ cup Hummus, p. 118, in whole wheat pita pocket with chopped tomatoes and lettuce; carrot sticks; apple

Dinner

1 cup pasta shells with ½ cup Velvety Cheeze Sauce, p. 123; tossed salad with Flax and Olive Vinaigrette, p. 74; Cheezy Garlic Bread, p. 53; 1 cup steamed kale

Snacks

¼ cup almonds; apricot juice

❦ *Day Two* ❦

Breakfast

Cold cereal or Maple-Walnut Granola, p. 39, with fortified nondairy milk and sliced banana; 6 ounces calcium-fortified orange juice; 2 slices whole wheat toast with fruit spread

Lunch

⅓ cup Happy Hen Salad, p. 120, on whole wheat bread; tossed salad with oil and vinegar dressing; 2 fresh apricots

Dinner

1 cup Bean & Barley Chowder, p. 56; 2 slices multi-grain bread; 1½ cups steamed broccoli and cauliflower drizzled with 2 teaspoons organic flax oil, served with lemon wedges

Snacks

Apple slices with 2 tablespoons Peanut Whip, p. 119

❦ *Day Three* ❦

Breakfast

2 Boston Brown Bread Muffins, p. 51;
6 ounces calcium-fortified orange juice;
1 cup fortified nondairy milk

Lunch

1 cup Bean & Barley Chowder, p. 56;
Salad with Classic Ranch Dressing, p. 73;
1 slice whole wheat bread; 2 dried figs

Dinner

2 Bean Burritos, p. 114; 1 cup cooked
Brown Rice, p. 92, drizzled with 1-2 teaspoons organic flax oil; 1 cup steamed kale
with fresh lemon juice

Snacks

Apple slices with 1 tablespoon almond
butter

❦ *Day Four* ❦

Breakfast

Swiss-Style Muesli, p. 37; 6 ounces grapefruit juice; 2 slices whole wheat toast with
fruit spread

Lunch

1 cup instant lentil soup; 1 slice whole
wheat bread; 2 kiwi

Dinner

1 cup spaghetti with prepared spaghetti
sauce; Cheezy Garlic Bread, p. 53;
1 cup steamed or braised collards;
½ cup canned apricots in juice

Snacks

1 Boston Brown Bread Muffin, p. 51;
1 cup fortified nondairy milk

❦ *Day Five* ❦

Breakfast

2 slices French Toast, p. 42, with Fruit and
Maple Blend, p. 46; 6 ounces calcium-fortified orange juice

Lunch

½ cup Garbanzo Sandwich Salad on
2 slices whole grain toast, p. 115; salad
with French dressing; apple

Dinner

Tofu Scrambola, p. 133; Slow-Baked
Tomatoes, p. 86; 1 cup steamed kale;
1 piece Down-Home Cornbread, p. 54

Snacks

Orange; bagel with fruit spread

❦ *Day Six* ❦

Breakfast

English muffin spread with 1 tablespoon
almond butter; Stewed Prunes, p. 44;
1 cup fortified nondairy milk

Lunch

½ cup Monster Mash spread, p. 111, on
2 slices whole wheat bread with lettuce;
carrot and celery sticks; pear

Dinner

Veggie burger on a whole wheat roll with
ketchup, tomato slices, and pickles; Steak
Fries, p. 81; 1 cup steamed or braised collards with fresh lemon juice; ½ cup
steamed carrots

Snacks

½ cup Maple Walnut Granola, p. 40, or
¼ cup trail mix; apple; 1 cup fortified
nondairy milk

❧ *Day Seven* ❧

Breakfast

Cream of Rice with Raisins, p. 34;
6 ounces calcium-fortified orange juice;
1 slice cinnamon raisin toast with
2 teaspoons Almond-Flax Butter, p. 45

Lunch

1 cup instant black bean soup; 2 slices
whole wheat bread; salad with oil and
vinegar dressing; carrot sticks

Dinner

Baked Potatoes Florentine, p. 150;
1 piece Down-Home Cornbread, p. 54;
1 cup steamed carrots; fresh pineapple (or
canned pineapple packed in juice)

Snacks

1 slice whole grain bread with 2 teaspoons
almond butter; 1 cup fortified vanilla
nondairy milk; banana

❧ *Day Nine* ❧

Breakfast

Hot Whole Wheat with Dates, p. 36;
6 ounces apple juice; 1 cup fortified
nondairy milk

Lunch

1 cup instant chili; 1 cup baked tortilla
chips; orange

Dinner

Roasted Vegetable Pizza with Tomato-
Tinged Tofu, p. 108; tossed salad with
Tomato-Garlic Dressing, p. 73

Snacks

Apple slices with 1 tablespoon almond
butter

❧ *Day Eight* ❧

Breakfast

Cinnamon-Apple Oatmeal, p. 33;
6 ounces calcium-fortified orange juice;
1 slice whole wheat toast with fruit butter

Lunch

½ cup North Country Bean Pâté, p. 117, in
whole wheat pita pocket; lettuce and tomato salad with oil and vinegar dressing; pear

Dinner

Garlic-Infused Smashed Potatoes, p. 90,
with Herbed Brown Gravy, p. 125; Crusty
Carrot Sticks, p. 86; Greens & Garlic,
p. 85; 1 slice multi-grain bread

Snacks

Stewed Prunes, p. 44; 1 cup fortified
nondairy milk

❧ *Day Ten* ❧

Breakfast

Bran flakes or Maple-Walnut Granola, p. 39,
with fortified nondairy milk and fresh blueberries; 6 ounces calcium-fortified orange
juice; 1 slice multi-grain toast with 2 teaspoons Almond-Flax Butter, p. 45

Lunch

Baked potato with salsa; salad with oil and
vinegar dressing; peach slices

Dinner

Mahvelous Millet Loaf, p. 152; 1 cup
steamed broccoli with 2 tablespoons No-
Cook Hollandaise Sauce, p. 80; sliced
beets; Apple Crisp, p. 159

Snacks

½ cup salt-free pretzels; pear; 1 cup fortified nondairy milk

❦ *Day Eleven* ❦

Breakfast

Tropical-Style Muesli, p. 38; 6 ounces calcium-fortified orange juice; 1 slice whole grain toast with 2 teaspoons almond butter

Lunch

Veggie burger on a whole wheat roll with ketchup, lettuce, and pickles; carrot sticks; banana

Dinner

Mushroom Barley Pilaf, p. 101; Brussels Sprouts Salad, p. 72; sliced tomatoes; ½ cup canned apricots

Snacks

Apple Crisp, p. 159; 1 cup fortified nondairy milk

❦ *Day Twelve* ❦

Breakfast

2 Applesauce Muffins, p. 48; 1 cup fortified nondairy milk; 6 ounces calcium-fortified orange juice

Lunch

Easy Baked Beans, p. 82; Coleslaw made with shredded cabbage, carrots and Low-Fat, Egg-Free Mayonnaise, p. 128; 1 cup baked tortilla chips

Dinner

Spinach and Garbanzo Curry, p. 143; 1 cup cooked Brown Rice, p. 92; carrot sticks; tossed salad with oil and vinegar dressing

Snacks

Rice cake with 2 tablespoons Peanut Whip, p. 119; fruit leather

❦ *Day Thirteen* ❦

Breakfast

½ grapefruit; toasted bagel with 1 tablespoon Almond-Flax Butter, p. 45; 1 cup fortified nondairy milk

Lunch

½ cup Hummus, p. 118, in whole wheat pita pocket with chopped tomatoes and lettuce; carrot sticks; apple

Dinner

Tofu Brochettes, p. 138; 1 cup cooked Quinoa, p. 95; Greens and Garlic, p. 85

Snacks

1 Applesauce Muffin, p. 48; 1 cup fortified nondairy milk

❦ *Day Fourteen* ❦

Breakfast

Oatmeal with Hot Cinnamon Apple Topping, p. 44; 1 cup fortified nondairy milk

Lunch

1 cup instant lentil soup; 1 slice whole wheat bread with 2 teaspoons tahini; pear

Dinner

Igor's Special, p. 145; tossed salad with oil and vinegar dressing; Rice 'n Raisin Puddin', p. 165

Snacks

Applesauce; bagel with fruit spread; ¼ cup soy nuts

Special Ingredients at a Glance

- **Balsamic vinegar** is an exquisitely flavored seasoning made from white Trebbiano grape juice that acquires a dark amber color and pungent sweetness after aging for three to thirty years in barrels made from various woods, such as red oak, chestnut, mulberry, and juniper. The finest balsamics are slightly sweet, heavy, mellow, and dark.

- **Brown rice vinegar** is a mild vinegar made from fermented rice. It is widely used in Asian cooking and adds a light, exotic flavor to sauces and dressings. Traditionally, the vinegar is brewed in earthenware crocks. It is then filtered and aged in casks until the flavor is mellow and the color is deep amber.

- **Bulgur** is hard red winter wheat that has been cracked and toasted. It comes in coarse, medium, and fine grinds. Bulgur cooks quickly, has a chewy meatlike texture, and a delicious nutty flavor.

- **Canola oil** has a mild taste and is ideal for recipes where blandness is desirable, such as for desserts, or where olive oil or other strong tasting oils would overpower delicate flavors.

- **Couscous** is a granular semolina, made from the same wheat that is used to make pasta. It is a staple of North African cuisine. Cooked couscous may be served with nondairy milk as a porridge, with a dressing as a salad, as a side dish similar to rice, as a grain to complement vegetable stews, or sweetened and mixed with fruit for breakfast or dessert. Couscous is available in natural food stores, Middle Eastern grocery stores, and many supermarkets. Whole wheat couscous is also available. It is cooked in the same manner as regular couscous, and the two may be interchanged measure for measure in recipes.

- **Extra-virgin olive oil** is one of the least processed oils. It is high in monounsaturated fat and has a rich olive flavor. Cold pressing produces the best olive oil because it yields a naturally low level of acidity. *Extra-virgin* means the oil is the result of the first pressing of the olives and is only one percent acid. It is the finest and fruitiest of the olive oils and is consequently the most expensive. Extra-virgin olive oil ranges in color from amber champagne to greenish-golden to bright green. In general, the deeper the color, the more intense the olive flavor. *Pure olive oil* and *olive oil* are produced from the second or third pressings of the same olives used to make extra-virgin oil. They are generally much paler in color, with a weak olive flavor and a very oily taste. Don't be fooled by olive oil labeled *light*—it has the same fat and calories as regular olive oil. What the term "light" refers to is the lighter color and fragrance and nondescript flavor resulting from an extremely fine filtration process. If you can't smell the olives, don't use the oil.

- **Flaxseeds** are rich in fiber and omega-3 fatty acids and make an excellent substitute for eggs in baking. To use for this purpose, finely grind one tablespoon of whole flaxseeds in an electric herb or coffee mill, or in a dry blender. Beat along with three to four tablespoons of water, and process until frothy and viscous. This will make the equivalent of one medium egg for use in baking. Use immediately, or store in the refrigerator for up to three days. Flaxseeds are available in natural food stores. They are highly perishable and should be stored in the freezer to prevent oxidation and rancidity.

- **Organic flaxseed oil** is an abundant source of omega-3 fatty acids, one of the essential fatty acids most often lacking in modern diets. Omega-3 fatty acids have been attributed with amazing healing and preventative properties. Using flax oil as a salad dressing and drizzling it over cooked foods, such as a baked potato, are the easiest and most nutritious ways to incorporate this essential fatty acid into your daily diet.

Because flax oil is prone to rancidity and highly susceptible to nutrient loss from exposure to air, light, and heat, special care must be taken when purchasing and storing it and when using it in recipes. Always keep flax oil in the refrigerator. It may also be kept in the freezer, which will extend its shelf life a few weeks. Recap it immediately after use, and return it to the refrigerator or freezer as soon as possible. Never heat flax oil or use it in cooking. Purchase only refrigerated flax oil in small quantities, about ten to twelve ounces at a time. It should come packaged in a light-impervious plastic or dark glass bottle that is stamped with a freshness date.

- **Millet** is an ancient grain native to the East Indies and North Africa. It has a tiny, round, yellowish seed, which resembles a mustard seed, and has a mild, slightly nutty flavor. Millet is gluten free, easily digested, and one of the least allergenic foods known. It contains abundant minerals, vitamins, protein, and fiber. When cooked, millet swells to a fluffy texture. Toasting it before cooking enhances the flavor and creates a more pilaf-like result. With extra water, millet can be cooked into a savory polenta or tasty breakfast porridge. It is available in natural food stores. Store at room temperature or in the freezer.

- **Miso** is a salty, flavorful, fermented soybean paste that often contains rice or barley. Some kinds of miso are made with other grains or beans. Used primarily as a seasoning, miso ranges from dark and strongly flavored to light, smooth, and delicately flavored. Light misos are generally sweeter and less salty than dark misos. Look for refrigerated, unpasteurized miso in natural food stores.

- **Naturally brewed soy sauce (tamari & shoyu)** is produced by the natural fermentation of soybeans, salt, water, and sometimes wheat. Naturally brewed soy sauce is called *shoyu* if wheat is used, *tamari* if it is not. The finest soy sauces are aged for a year or longer. With time, you will develop as discriminating a taste for naturally brewed soy sauce as some people have for fine wine. Store it at room temperature or in the refrigerator for optimum flavor. It will keep indefinitely. For a lower sodium content, look for reduced-sodium or "lite" soy sauce.

- **Nondairy milk** refers to any low-fat, creamy, plant-based beverage including soymilk, rice milk, oat milk, mixed grain milk, and some nut milks. To reduce the fat in higher-fat nut milks, thin them with water using two parts nut milk to one part water. Nondairy milks are available in natural food stores, fresh in the deli or dairy case or in aseptic packages on the shelf, and in many supermarkets. Unless otherwise specified, use only the plain unflavored product in recipes, and look for those that have been fortified with calcium, vitamin D, and vitamin B12. Taste various milks from different manufacturers to find the brands you most prefer. Opened packages of nondairy milks will keep for about a week.

- **Nutritional yeast** is a natural whole plant grown as a food crop. It is prized for its delicious, nutty taste and high nutritional content. When mixed with certain seasonings, nutritional yeast can also impart a cheesy taste or a poultry-like flavor. Most nutritional yeasts are a concentrated source of protein, a good source of B-complex vitamins, contain no fat, and have few calories. Red

Star Vegetarian Support Formula nutritional yeast also has vitamin B12 added, an important nutrient in vegan diets. If you are unable to locate Red Star Vegetarian Support Formula nutritional yeast in your area, it may be ordered from The Mail Order Catalog, Box 180, Summertown, TN 38483. For current price information, call 1-800-695-2241.

- **Quinoa** is a small, quick-cooking, gluten-free grain that is native to the Andes. Its small, disk-shaped seeds look like a cross between sesame seeds and millet. It has more calcium than cow's milk, is high in protein, rich in minerals, and easy to digest. Rinse well under cold water before cooking to remove its bitter coating. Store in the freezer.

- **Salsa** is a condiment or dip featuring tomatoes, chilies, and cilantro. Store opened jars in the refrigerator.

- **Sugar,** in the recipes in this book, refers to sweeteners made from unrefined and unbleached cane sugar (such as Florida's Crystals), evaporated sugar-cane juice (such as Sucanat), or turbinado sugar (also known as "raw" sugar). Although white sugar will work fine in any of the recipes that call for sugar, the less refined products are preferable and highly recommended.

- **Tahini** is a paste made by grinding raw or lightly toasted whole or hulled sesame seeds. It is light tan in color and rich and creamy like peanut butter. The consistency of tahini varies from brand to brand, with some being creamier and smoother and others being more oily or dry. Seek out tahini made from organically grown sesame seeds for the best flavor and quality. Pour off the excess oil that rises to the top. Stir well, and store in the refrigerator in an airtight container.

- **Tempeh** (pronounced TEM-pay) is a savory, protein-rich food made from split and hulled cooked soybeans and grains that are combined with a culture and incubated. It has a distinctive taste, somewhat similar to mushrooms, and a succulent, chewy texture. Tempeh is excellent steamed, baked, or sautéed, and makes an ideal substitute for meat in dishes like tacos, stew, and chili. Tempeh can also be marinated and grilled like a burger. It is available refrigerated or in the frozen foods section of natural food stores.

- **Tofu (regular)**, also known as Chinese tofu, is packed in water and is generally available in plastic tubs in the refrigerated section of your natural food store.

You may also find it in the produce section of many supermarkets. Look for tofu that has been processed with calcium salts, which will provide you with the highest calcium content.

- **Tofu (silken)**, also known as Japanese tofu, is a smooth, creamy, delicate tofu that is excellent for blending into sauces, dips, cream soups, and puddings. It is often available in special aseptic packaging, which allows storage without refrigeration for up to a year. After opening, aseptically packaged tofu must be refrigerated. One popular brand, Mori-Nu, is available in most grocery stores. Look for the reduced-fat, or "lite," variety. Other brands of silken tofu are available in the refrigerated section of supermarkets and natural food stores.

- **Umeboshi plum paste** is the mashed meat of umeboshi plums, a salty, Japanese seasoning made from whole Japanese plums, an herb called beefsteak leaf (red shiso), and sea salt. This pickle is then fermented for a minimum of eighteen months, resulting in a condiment that is at once salty and sour, with a deep fuschia color. This convenient seasoning paste must be diluted with a liquid for even distribution in recipes. Store it in a tightly sealed container in the refrigerator. It will keep for several months.

- **Umeboshi plum vinegar** is a bright purple-pink vinegar made from the liquid used to pickle umeboshi plums (see above). It has a gloriously intense tart flavor and a strong salty taste. Store at room temperature.

CHAPTER 1

RISE & SHINE
BREAKFASTS

ORANGE-APRICOT OATMEAL

Yield: 2 servings

A chewy and satisfying hot cereal, with just a hint of sweetness. Dried apricots are an excellent source of vitamin A, iron, and potassium. Seek out organic dried apricots; they will be a deep orange-brown color. Avoid ones that are bright orange because they will have been treated with sulfur dioxide.

1 cup old-fashioned rolled oats

1¼ cups cold water

½ cup orange juice

2 Tablespoons chopped dried apricots

¼ teaspoon nutmeg

Tiny pinch of salt

Flavoring options:

Sweetener of your choice

2 teaspoons organic flax oil

2 Tablespoons chopped walnuts, almonds, or pecans, raw or lightly pan toasted

1. Combine all the ingredients, except the flavoring options, in a medium saucepan, and bring to a boil. Cover and reduce the heat to low. Simmer 5 minutes, stirring once or twice.

2. Remove from the heat, leave covered, and let sit for 2 to 5 minutes.

3. Stir in the sweetener and flax oil, if using. Sprinkle 1 tablespoon nuts over each serving, if desired.

Per serving: Calories 214, Protein 8 g, Fat 3 g, Carbohydrates 38 g

Tip: To pan toast the nuts, lightly roast them in a dry skillet over medium heat, stirring often, until fragrant and golden brown.

CINNAMON-APPLE OATMEAL

Yield: 2 servings

Old-fashioned rolled oats make a hearty morning meal. If you prefer, use dates or raisins instead of, or in addition to, the dried apples.

1. Combine all the ingredients, except the flavoring options, in a medium saucepan, and bring to a boil. Cover and reduce the heat to low. Simmer 5 minutes, stirring once or twice.

2. Remove from the heat, leave covered, and let sit for 2 to 5 minutes.

3. Stir in the sweetener and flax oil, if using. Sprinkle 1 tablespoon nuts over each serving, if desired.

1 cup old-fashioned rolled oats

1¼ cups cold water

½ cup apple juice

2 Tablespoons chopped dried apples

¼ teaspoon cinnamon

Tiny pinch of salt

Flavoring options:

Sweetener of your choice

2 teaspoons organic flax oil

2 Tablespoons chopped walnuts, almonds, or pecans, raw or lightly pan toasted

Per serving: Calories 204,
Protein 8 g, Fat 3 g,
Carbohydrates 36 g

CREAM OF RICE WITH RAISINS

Yield: 2 servings

A *soothing and healthful hot cereal.*

❧

½ cup brown rice cream
(see Tips next page)
1¾ cups water
¼ cup raisins
¼ teaspoon salt

Flavoring options:

Sweetener of your choice
2 teaspoons organic flax oil
1 teaspoon vanilla extract
Pinch of cinnamon for
garnish
Nondairy milk

1. Combine all the ingredients, except the flavoring options, in a medium saucepan, and bring to a boil, stirring constantly. Cover and reduce the heat to low. Simmer, stirring occasionally, until the rice is tender, about 20 to 30 minutes. For less stirring and sticking, transfer the mixture to a double boiler to finish cooking after the cereal comes to a boil.

2. Remove from the heat and stir in the flavoring options of your choice. Top each serving with a sprinkle of cinnamon, if desired. Serve hot with nondairy milk.

Per serving: Calories 166,
Protein 3 g, Fat 0 g,
Carbohydrates 39 g

Tips: *Finely cracked rice is called "rice cream." Brown rice cream is available commercially from natural food companies under a variety of different names. (For example, a popular brand from Arrowhead Mills is called Rice & Shine.) Store rice cream in an airtight container in the refrigerator or freezer. You can use it directly from the freezer without defrosting.*

If you cannot find packaged cracked brown rice, you can easily make it yourself at home. Rinse the rice well. Transfer it to a saucepan, place over medium heat, and stir almost constantly until the rice is dry. Remove from the heat and let cool completely. Place the cooled rice in a dry blender, and grind into a fine meal. If you make this recipe often, you may want to wash, dry, and grind a large quantity of rice, and store it in airtight containers in the refrigerator or freezer.

If the cereal sticks to the bottom of your saucepan, slip a flame tamer (also called a heat diffuser) underneath the pan while cooking.

Hot Whole Wheat with Dates, Prunes, or Apricots

Yield: 2 servings

This satisfying porridge includes the bran and germ of the whole wheat berry. Unlike most commercial hot wheat cereals, which are robbed of the grain's natural fiber and nutrition, leaving behind a stripped white product, this wholesome porridge is a beautiful earthy brown.

1¾ cups water

½ cup bulgur

¼ cup chopped pitted dates, prunes, or apricots

Pinch of salt

Flavoring options:

Sweetener of your choice

2 teaspoons organic flax oil

1 teaspoon vanilla extract

¼ teaspoon nutmeg

Nondairy milk

1. Combine all the ingredients, except the flavoring options, in a medium saucepan, and bring to a boil, stirring constantly. Cover and reduce the heat to low. Simmer, stirring occasionally, until the bulgur is tender, about 20 to 30 minutes. For less stirring and sticking, transfer the mixture to a double boiler to finish cooking after the cereal comes to a boil.

2. Remove from the heat and stir in the flavoring options of your choice. Serve hot with nondairy milk, if desired.

Tips: Bulgur is available in natural food stores.

If the cereal sticks to the bottom of your saucepan, slip a flame tamer (also called a heat diffuser) underneath the pan while cooking.

Per serving: Calories 287, Protein 9 g, Fat 0 g, Carbohydrates 62 g

36

SWISS-STYLE MUESLI

Yield: 2 servings

*T*his recipe is a variation of the original Swiss cereal created as part of a healing system based on a diet high in raw foods. The texture is somewhat similar to hot porridge; however, muesli is not cooked and is served cold. The premise is that soaking grains, nuts, and seeds overnight renders them easier to digest. In the morning, you simply stir in fresh fruit, and breakfast is ready to be served.

1. Combine the oats, raisins, nuts, and cinnamon in a medium bowl.

2. Stir together the milk and juice concentrate. Pour over the fruit and nut mixture, and stir to mix thoroughly. Cover and refrigerate overnight.

3. In the morning, grate or finely chop the fresh fruit, and add it to the muesli.

¾ cup old-fashioned rolled oats

2 Tablespoons raisins

2 Tablespoons chopped nuts or sunflower seeds

¼ teaspoon ground cinnamon

1 cup plain or vanilla nondairy milk

2 tablespoons frozen fruit juice concentrate, thawed

1 small apple or pear (peel if it is not organic)

Tips: *Sliced banana, peaches, fresh berries, or other fresh fruit may used in place of, or in addition to, the apple or pear. This recipe is easily doubled.*

Per serving: Calories 304, Protein 10 g, Fat 8 g, Carbohydrates 46 g

TROPICAL-STYLE MUESLI

Yield: 2 servings

A unique blend of pineapple and banana lend an unusual twist to this make-ahead breakfast.

¾ cup old-fashioned rolled oats

¼ teaspoon cardamom

8-ounce can unsweetened crushed pineapple packed in juice

½ cup plain or vanilla nondairy milk

1 small banana, sliced

2 Tablespoons chopped nuts or sunflower seeds

1. Combine the oats and cardamom in a medium bowl. Stir in the pineapple and milk, and mix thoroughly. Cover and refrigerate overnight.

2. In the morning, stir in the sliced banana and nuts or seeds.

Per serving: Calories 283, Protein 9 g, Fat 7 g, Carbohydrates 43 g

Tips: *Sliced peaches, fresh berries, or other fresh fruit may used in addition to the banana. This recipe is easily doubled.*

MAPLE-WALNUT GRANOLA

Yield: about 10 cups

Serve this crunchy, satisfying cereal with lots of chopped fresh fruit or berries and plenty of low-fat nondairy milk. This recipe makes a large quantity, but it will keep for a long time in the refrigerator, so there's no excuse to skip breakfast.

1. Combine the oats, barley flour, walnuts, sunflower seeds, and salt in a large bowl. In a separate bowl, whisk together the maple syrup, juice concentrate, oil, and vanilla. Pour over the dry ingredients, and mix thoroughly until evenly moistened.

2. Preheat the oven to 325°F. Divide the mixture between 2 large pans, spreading it out into a 1-inch-thick layer. Bake until golden brown, about 50 to 60 minutes. Stir well every 15 minutes, and spread the mixture back to a 1-inch-thick layer before returning it to the oven.

3. When the granola is finished baking, remove it from the oven and stir in the raisins while it is still hot. The steam from the hot cereal will help plump the raisins. Let cool completely. Store in airtight containers in the refrigerator.

6 cups old-fashioned rolled oats

1 cup barley flour (See Tips below)

1 cup coarsely chopped walnuts

1 cup raw sunflower seeds

½ teaspoon salt

1 cup pure maple syrup

½ cup frozen apple juice concentrate, thawed,

¼ cup canola oil

2 teaspoons vanilla extract

1 cup raisins

Tips: Barley flour is available in natural food stores. Store it in an airtight container in the freezer. It will keep for several months.

Replace or supplement the raisins with any chopped dried fruit of your choice. Good selections are dried apricots, dates, prunes, pears, apples, and figs. Try a mixture of fruit, or use different fruits each time you make the recipe.

Per ⅓ cup: Calories 199, Protein 5 g, Fat 7 g, Carbohydrates 28 g

FLAXJACKS

Yield: about 12 pancakes

*T*hese tender pancakes are great for leisurely mornings when you don't need to rush. They are light and fluffy and utterly fabulous. Try them topped with applesauce, fruit-sweetened jam, or Fruit & Maple Blend, p. 46, for a very special treat.

❧

1 cup whole wheat pastry flour

2 teaspoons double-acting non-aluminum baking powder (such as Rumford)

Pinch of salt

1 Tablespoon flaxseeds

¼ cup water

¾ cup plain nondairy milk

1 Tablespoon canola oil, plus extra as needed for cooking

1 Tablespoon sugar

½ teaspoon vanilla extract

1. Combine the flour, baking powder, and salt in a medium bowl.

2. Place the flaxseeds in a dry blender, and grind them into a powder. Add the water and blend until a gummy mixture is achieved, about 30 seconds. Add the milk, oil, sugar, and vanilla extract, and process until frothy and well blended. Pour into the flour mixture, and stir just until everything is evenly moistened.

3. Lightly oil a large skillet or mist it with nonstick cooking spray, and place it over medium-high heat. Spoon the batter into the hot skillet using about 2 tablespoons for each pancake. Cook until bubbles pop through the top of the pancakes and the bottoms are golden brown, about 2 to 3 minutes. Turn the pancakes over, and cook until they are golden and cooked through, about 1 minute longer.

Tips: *Be sure to add a bit more canola oil to the skillet between each batch to prevent the pancakes from sticking to the pan.*

To keep the finished pancakes warm while the remainder cook, place them on a baking sheet in a 300°F oven. This way you can serve the pancakes hot all at the same time, and no one has to wait.

Per flaxjack: Calories 57, Protein 2 g, Fat 2 g, Carbohydrates 8 g

Banana Buckwheat Pancakes

Yield: about 16 pancakes

*B*uckwheat adds a unique hearty flavor to these satisfying griddle cakes. Serve them with warm, homemade applesauce, fresh fruit, fruit-sweetened preserves, or good old maple syrup.

1. Combine the flours, baking powder, baking soda, and salt in a medium bowl.

2. Combine the banana, milk, maple syrup, oil, and vinegar in a separate small bowl, and beat them together using a fork. Pour into the dry ingredients, and stir with a wooden spoon. The batter will be slightly lumpy.

3. Lightly oil a large skillet or mist it with nonstick cooking spray, and place it over medium-high heat. Spoon the batter into the hot skillet using 2 level tablespoons for each pancake. Cook until the bottoms are brown and the tops are bubbly, adjusting the heat as necessary. Carefully loosen the pancakes, and turn them over using a metal spatula. Cook the second side briefly, just until golden.

½ cup whole wheat pastry flour

½ cup buckwheat flour

½ teaspoon double-acting non-aluminum baking powder (such as Rumford)

¼ teaspoon baking soda

Pinch of salt

1 medium, ripe banana, mashed

1 cup plain nondairy milk

2 Tablespoons pure maple syrup

2 teaspoons canola oil, plus extra as needed for cooking

2 teaspoons apple cider vinegar

Tips: *Be sure to add a bit more canola oil to the skillet between each batch to prevent the pancakes from sticking to the pan.*

To keep the finished pancakes warm while the remainder cook, place them on a baking sheet in a 300°F oven. This way you can serve the pancakes hot all at the same time, and no one has to wait.

Per pancake: Calories 47,
Protein 1 g, Fat 0 g,
Carbohydrates 9 g

ORANGE-OAT PANCAKES

Yield: about 16 pancakes

*T*hese pancakes have a delicate orange flavor that is nicely complemented by Hot Cinnamon Apple Topping, p. 44, or Apple-Maple Fusion, p. 46.

❧

1⅓ cups whole wheat pastry flour

⅔ cup old-fashioned rolled oats

2 teaspoons double-acting non-aluminum baking powder (such as Rumford)

½ teaspoon baking soda

1 cup plain nondairy milk

¼ cup applesauce

3 Tablespoons frozen orange juice concentrate, thawed

1. Combine the flour, rolled oats, baking powder, and baking soda in a medium bowl.

2. Combine the milk, applesauce, and juice concentrate in a separate small bowl, and beat them together using a fork. Pour into the dry ingredients, and stir with a wooden spoon. The batter will be slightly lumpy.

3. Oil a large skillet or mist it with nonstick cooking spray, and place it over medium-high heat. Spoon the batter into the hot skillet using 2 level tablespoons for each pancake. Cook until the bottoms are brown, adjusting the heat as necessary. Carefully loosen the pancakes, and turn them over using a metal spatula. Cook the second side briefly, just until golden.

Tips: *Be sure to add a bit more canola oil to the skillet between each batch to prevent the pancakes from sticking to the pan.*

To keep the finished pancakes warm while the remainder cook, place them on a baking sheet in a 300°F oven. This way you can serve the pancakes hot all at the same time, and no one has to wait.

Per pancake: Calories 60, Protein 2 g, Fat 0 g, Carbohydrates 11 g

FRENCH TOAST

Yield: 6 pieces

Serve warm with applesauce, fruit-sweetened preserves, Fruit & Maple Blend, p. 46, or buttery-tasting Flaxen Maple Syrup, p. 45.

1. Place the flour, nutritional yeast flakes, salt, cinnamon, and nutmeg in a medium bowl, and stir with a dry whisk until well blended. Pour the milk into the flour mixture, and whisk vigorously until well blended. Let the batter sit for 10 minutes.

2. Oil a skillet or griddle, and place it over medium-high heat. Mix the batter again. Dip the bread slices, one at a time, into the batter, making sure that each piece is well saturated. Cook 3 to 5 minutes, or until the bottom is lightly brown, then turn over and cook the other side until golden brown.

¼ cup whole wheat pastry flour

1 teaspoon nutritional yeast flakes

¼ teaspoon salt

Pinch of cinnamon and nutmeg

1 cup plain or vanilla nondairy milk

6 slices whole grain bread

Tip: This french toast tends to stick to the pan during cooking. Use a nonstick pan for the best results, or be sure to oil the pan well between batches.

Per piece: Calories 81, Protein 4 g, Fat 2 g, Carbohydrates 13 g

STEWED PRUNES

Yield: 1½ cups

*M**ost people think of prunes as nature's laxative. True as that may be, they are also quite delicious. Serve them hot or cold, unadorned or topped with plain or vanilla nondairy milk. Stewed prunes also make a tasty topping for hot oatmeal or French Toast, page 43.*

❧

1 cup pitted prunes

1 cup water

Per ¼ cup: Calories 64,
Protein 1 g, Fat 0 g,
Carbohydrates 15 g

Combine the prunes and water in a small saucepan, and bring to a boil. Reduce the heat to medium, cover, and simmer until the prunes are tender, about 20 minutes.

HOT CINNAMON APPLE TOPPING

Yield: 2 servings

*T**his chunky sauce makes a tempting topping for pancakes, French Toast, p. 43, or plain oatmeal. It also makes a luscious topping for low-fat vanilla nondairy frozen dessert. The sauce has a gentle sweetness that is mellow but not cloying.*

1 Granny Smith apple, peeled, cored, and cut into 12 equal slices

⅔ cup frozen apple juice concentrate, thawed

2 Tablespoons raisins or chopped dates

1 teaspoon fresh lemon juice

¼ teaspoon cinnamon

Combine all the ingredients in a small saucepan, and bring to a boil. Reduce the heat to medium-low, and simmer, stirring occasionally, until the apple is soft but not mushy. Serve hot or warm.

Per serving: Calories 221,
Protein 1 g, Fat 0 g,
Carbohydrates 53 g

ALMOND-FLAX BUTTER

Yield: about ½ cup

*U*se this golden spread as a replacement for dairy butter on toasted bread or bagels. Although it is rich in omega-3 fatty acids, it is also high in fat, so use it sparingly and judiciously.

1. If your almonds do not have skins, you can skip this step. If your almonds do have skins, they will need to be blanched and peeled. Place the almonds in a small saucepan, and cover them with water. Bring to a boil, reduce the heat slightly, and simmer for 2 minutes. Drain the almonds in a colander, and rinse them under cold water. Pop off the skins by pinching the base of each almond between your thumb and forefinger. Pat the almonds dry.

2. Grind the almonds into a meal in a food processor fitted with a metal blade. Add the oil 1 tablespoon at a time, and process until creamy. Season with salt. Store in an airtight container in the refrigerator. This will keep for at least a week.

½ cup raw almonds

3 Tablespoons organic flax oil

Pinch of salt

Per tablespoon: Calories 101
Protein 2 g, Fat 8 g,
Carbohydrates 2 g

FLAXEN MAPLE SYRUP

Yield: about ½ cup

*F*lax oil adds a luscious buttery taste and essential omega-3 fatty acids to this sweet and simple recipe.

Place the maple syrup and flax oil in a small bowl. Whisk vigorously until well blended.

½ cup pure maple syrup

2 teaspoons organic flax oil

Per ¼ cup: Calories 240,
Protein 0 g, Fat 4 g,
Carbohydrates 50 g

45

FRUIT & MAPLE BLEND

Yield: about ½ cup

*T*his luscious mixture is an ideal topping for pancakes, French Toast, p. 43, and hot cereal.

❧

¼ cup pure maple syrup

¼ cup berries, or peeled and minced fresh fruit

Combine the maple syrup and fruit in a small bowl or measuring cup and stir together until well combined. For a smoother consistency, combine the mixture in a blender, and process just until lightly blended.

Tip: *This recipe is easily doubled, tripled, or quadrupled. It's great when you're cooking for a crowd and want an easy, delicious topping that tastes really special but doesn't require much work.*

Tip: *Fruit-sweetened preserves may be substituted for the fresh fruit, if preferred. If the preserves are very thick, stir them well; then thin with a little water, if necessary, before combining with the maple syrup.*

Per ¼ cup: Calories 110, Protein 0 g, Fat 0 g, Carbohydrates 28 g

APPLE-MAPLE FUSION

Yield: about ½ cup

*P*ure maple syrup is unquestionably delicious, but it's also high in calories and frequently quite expensive. To reduce the cost to your waistline and your wallet, try this fabulous blend. It is so easy to make, adds a bit of extra nutrition, and extends the maple syrup while retaining all of its magnificent flavor.

¼ cup pure maple syrup

¼ cup unsweetened applesauce

Stir together the maple syrup and applesauce until well blended. Serve at room temperature or warm briefly over low heat.

Per ¼ cup: Calories 113, Protein 0 g, Fat 0 g, Carbohydrates 29 g

Tip: *This recipe is easily doubled, tripled, or quadrupled. It's great when you're in a hurry or have guests because it's effortless!*

CHAPTER II

MUFFINS &
QUICK BREADS

APPLESAUCE MUFFINS

Yield: 12 muffins

*M*_{*oist and sweet, these muffins are chock-full of raisins and brimming with home-style flavor.*}

❧

2 cups whole wheat pastry flour

½ cup raisins or currants

2 teaspoons double-acting, non-aluminum baking powder (such as Rumford)

1 teaspoon baking soda

1 teaspoon cinnamon

2 Tablespoons flaxseeds

½ cup water

1 cup applesauce

¼ cup pure maple syrup

¼ cup canola oil

1 Tablespoon fresh lemon juice

2 teaspoons vanilla extract

1. Preheat the oven to 375°F. Lightly oil the bottoms and sides of 12 muffin cups with canola oil or nonstick cooking spray.

2. Combine the flour, raisins or currants, baking powder, baking soda, and cinnamon in a large bowl, and stir with a wire whisk until well blended.

3. Place the flaxseeds in a dry blender and grind them into a powder. Add the water and blend until a gummy mixture is achieved, about 30 seconds. Add the remaining ingredients and process until well blended. Pour into the flour mixture, and stir just until everything is evenly moistened. The batter will be stiff.

4. Quickly spoon into the prepared muffin cups, filling each cup almost to the top. The cups will be quite full. Bake immediately on the center shelf of the oven until a toothpick inserted in the center of a muffin comes out clean, about 18 to 20 minutes.

5. Cool the muffins in the pan on a rack for 2 minutes. Run a table knife around the rim of each muffin, then carefully loosen the muffins and turn them out onto a cooling rack. Serve warm, or cool completely before storing in an airtight container in the refrigerator for future use.

Per muffin: Calories 159,
Protein 3 g, Fat 5 g,
Carbohydrates 25 g

BANANA NUT MUFFINS

Yield: 12 muffins

These dense, flavorful muffins are sweetened only with a little fruit juice concentrate and the rich, natural sweetness of ripe bananas. They are a great way to use up bananas that are becoming a tad too ripe.

1. Preheat the oven to 375°F. Lightly oil the bottoms and sides of 12 muffin cups with canola oil or nonstick cooking spray.

2. Combine the flour, walnuts, raisins or currants, baking powder, and baking soda in a large bowl, and stir with a wire whisk until well blended.

3. Place the flaxseeds in a dry blender, and grind them into a powder. Add the water and blend until a gummy mixture is achieved, about 30 seconds. Add the remaining ingredients and process until well blended. Pour into the flour mixture, and stir just until everything is evenly moistened.

4. Quickly spoon the batter into the prepared muffin cups, filling each cup almost to the top. The cups will be quite full. Bake immediately on the center shelf of the oven until a toothpick inserted in the center of a muffin comes out clean, about 18 to 20 minutes.

5. Cool the muffins in the pan on a rack for 2 minutes. Run a table knife around the rim of each muffin, then carefully loosen the muffins, and turn them out onto a cooling rack. Serve warm or cool completely before storing in an airtight container in the refrigerator for future use.

2 cups whole wheat pastry flour

⅓ cup chopped walnuts

⅓ cup raisins or currants (optional)

2 teaspoons double-acting, non-aluminum baking powder (such as Rumford)

1 teaspoon baking soda

2 Tablespoons flaxseeds

½ cup water

1 cup mashed ripe banana

⅓ cup frozen apple juice concentrate, thawed

¼ cup canola oil

2 teaspoons vanilla extract

Per muffin: Calories 158,
Protein 3 g, Fat 7 g,
Carbohydrates 20 g

49

MUFFINS THAT TASTE LIKE DONUTS

Yield: 12 muffins

Surprise, surprise—you can have your donuts and eat them too! Moist and sweet, these muffins are sure to satisfy any craving for powdered donuts, with just a mere fraction of the fat and calories donuts typically contain.

Topping:

2 Tablespoons sugar

½ teaspoon cinnamon

Dry ingredients:

2 cups whole wheat pastry flour

¼ cup sugar

2 teaspoons double-acting, non-aluminum baking powder (such as Rumford)

1 teaspoon baking soda

½ teaspoon nutmeg

¼ teaspoon cinnamon

Wet ingredients:

2 Tablespoons flaxseeds

½ cup water

½ cup applesauce

½ cup plain nondairy milk

3 Tablespoons pure maple syrup

3 Tablespoons canola oil

1 Tablespoon fresh lemon juice

Per muffin: Calories 148, Protein 3 g, Fat 4 g, Carbohydrates 24 g

1. Preheat the oven to 375°F. Lightly oil the bottoms and sides of 12 muffin cups with canola oil or nonstick cooking spray.

2. Combine the sugar and cinnamon for the topping in a small bowl, and set aside. Combine the dry ingredients in a large bowl, and stir with a wire whisk until well blended.

3. Place the flaxseeds in a dry blender and grind them into a powder. Add the water and blend until a gummy mixture is achieved, about 30 seconds. Add the remaining wet ingredients, and process until well blended. Pour into the flour mixture, and stir just until everything is evenly moistened.

4. Quickly spoon the batter into the prepared muffin cups, filling each cup almost to the top. The cups will be quite full. Sprinkle the surface of the muffins evenly with the reserved topping, using about ½ teaspoon per muffin. Bake immediately on the center shelf of the oven until a toothpick inserted in the center of a muffin comes out clean, about 18 to 20 minutes.

5. Cool the muffins in the pan on a rack for 2 minutes. Run a table knife around the rim of each muffin. Carefully loosen and pry them out. Transfer them to a cooling rack, taking care not to shake off the topping. Serve warm or cool completely before storing in an airtight container in the refrigerator for future use.

Boston Brown Bread Muffins

Yield: 12 muffins

These famous New England-style muffins are dark, dense, and delicious.

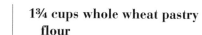

1. Preheat the oven to 375°F. Lightly oil the bottoms and sides of 12 muffin cups with canola oil or nonstick cooking spray.
2. Combine the flour, cornmeal, currants, baking powder, and baking soda in a large bowl, and stir with a wire whisk until well blended.
3. Place the flaxseeds in a dry blender and grind them into a powder. Add the water and blend until a gummy mixture is achieved, about 30 seconds. Add the remaining wet ingredients, and process until well blended. Pour into the flour mixture, and stir just until everything is evenly moistened.
4. Quickly spoon the batter into the prepared muffin cups, filling each cup almost to the top. The cups will be quite full. Bake immediately on the center shelf of the oven until a toothpick inserted in the center of a muffin comes out clean, about 18 to 20 minutes.
5. Cool the muffins in the pan on a rack for 2 minutes. Run a table knife around the rim of each muffin, then carefully loosen the muffins and turn them out onto a cooling rack. Serve warm, or cool completely before storing in an airtight container in the refrigerator for future use.

Tip: *Measure out the oil before the molasses. The coating of oil that remains in the measuring cup will allow the molasses to slide out easily.*

1¾ cups whole wheat pastry flour

½ cup yellow cornmeal

½ cup currants or raisins

2 teaspoons double-acting, non-aluminum baking powder (such as Rumford)

2 teaspoons baking soda

2 Tablespoons flaxseeds

½ cup water

½ cup plain nondairy milk or water

½ cup applesauce

¼ cup canola oil

¼ cup blackstrap molasses

Per muffin: Calories 167, Protein 3 g, Fat 5 g, Carbohydrates 26 g

51

DATE & NUT BREAD

Yield: 1 loaf (10 to 12 servings)

*T*his wholesome quick bread is magnificent unaccompanied, but if you prefer a spread, try applesauce or fruit-sweetened jam.

Dry ingredients:

2 cups whole wheat pastry flour

2 teaspoons double-acting, non-aluminum baking powder (such as Rumford)

1 teaspoon baking soda

Wet ingredients:

1 cup applesauce

½ cup plain nondairy milk

¼ cup pure maple syrup

2 Tablespoons frozen orange juice concentrate, thawed

2 Tablespoons canola oil

1 teaspoon vanilla extract

½ cup chopped dates

½ cup coarsely chopped walnuts

Per serving: Calories 189,
Protein 4 g, Fat 6 g,
Carbohydrates 29 g

1. Preheat the oven to 350°F. Lightly oil an 8½ x 4½-inch loaf pan, or mist it with nonstick cooking spray.

2. Combine the dry ingredients in a large bowl, and stir until well combined. Place the wet ingredients in a separate bowl, and stir until well combined. Pour the wet ingredients into the dry ingredients. Mix just until the dry ingredients are evenly moistened. Fold in the dates and walnuts, distributing them evenly.

3. Pour the batter into the prepared loaf pan. Bake on the center rack of the oven until a toothpick inserted in the center comes out clean, about 50 minutes.

4. Turn the bread out of the loaf pan onto a cooling rack, and carefully turn it upright. Cool completely before slicing or storing. Store in an airtight container in the refrigerator for future use.

Variations: For **Cranberry-Nut Bread,** *replace the dates with ½ cup fresh or frozen cranberries. For the best results, coarsely chop the cranberries by pulsing them briefly in a food processor fitted with a metal blade.*

For **Prune & Nut Bread,** *replace the dates with ½ cup chopped, pitted prunes.*

CHEEZY GARLIC BREAD

Yield: 12 to 16 servings

Garlic bread is the perfect companion to soups, salads, and pasta. It also makes a popular party bread. Although it's effortless to make, everyone will be impressed with your exceptional culinary skills!

1. Preheat the oven to 425°F. Slice the bread in half vertically and then horizontally to make four equal pieces. Spread each piece with about 1 tablespoon of olive oil, drizzling it evenly all over. Use a table knife to spread it out to the edges of the bread.

2. Using your fingers, dust the garlic powder lightly but evenly over the oiled bread. Then sprinkle on the nutritional yeast flakes.

3. Place the bread on a dry baking sheet, and bake on the center rack of the oven just until golden brown and crisp, about 10 to 12 minutes. Dust with paprika before serving, if desired. Serve hot.

1 large loaf Italian bread

3 to 4 Tablespoons extra-virgin olive oil, as needed

½ to 1 teaspoon garlic powder, as needed

2 to 4 Tablespoons nutritional yeast flakes, as needed

Paprika for garnish (optional)

Per serving: Calories 115, Protein 4 g, Fat 5 g, Carbohydrates 14 g

53

Down-Home Cornbread

Yield: 1 loaf (9 servings)

*W*ith just a hint of sweetness, this highly adaptable cornbread makes a great breakfast treat. If you add a few savory seasonings, however, you can easily transform it into a very special dinner or soup accompaniment.

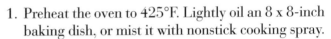

1 cup silken tofu

½ cup frozen apple juice concentrate, thawed

½ cup water

¼ cup canola oil

1 cup whole wheat pastry flour

⅔ cup yellow cornmeal

2 teaspoons double-acting, non-aluminum baking powder (such as Rumford)

1 teaspoon baking soda

½ teaspoon salt

1. Preheat the oven to 425°F. Lightly oil an 8 x 8-inch baking dish, or mist it with nonstick cooking spray.

2. Place the tofu, juice concentrate, water, and in a blender, and process into a smooth, creamy emulsion.

3. Place the remaining ingredients in a medium bowl, and stir together until well combined. Pour the blended mixture into the dry ingredients, and stir just until evenly moistened. The batter will be stiff. Immediately spoon into the prepared pan. Bake until golden brown, about 20 to 25 minutes. Serve hot.

Variations:

For **Maple Cornbread**, *replace the juice concentrate with an equal amount of pure maple syrup.*

For **Orange Cornbread**, *replace the apple juice concentrate with an equal amount of orange juice concentrate.*

For **Blueberry Cornbread**, *fold 1 cup fresh blueberries, rinsed and patted dry, into the batter.*

For **Spicy Cornbread**, *stir ½ cup sliced scallions, ¼ cup chopped green chilies, and 1 teaspoon cumin into the batter.*

For **Extra-Corny Cornbread**, *stir 1 cup whole corn kernels into the batter.*

Per serving: Calories 175,
Protein 4 g, Fat 8 g,
Carbohydrates 24 g

CHAPTER III

SATISFYING SOUPS & STEWS

BEAN & BARLEY CHOWDER

Yield: about 2 quarts

*B*arley is an excellent source of soluble fiber, which is beneficial for reducing blood cholesterol levels. This thick and hearty soup is a scrumptious way to include barley in your diet. The longer you cook the soup, the thicker, creamier, and richer tasting it becomes.

❦

8 cups water or vegetable stock

1 cup dry baby lima beans, soaked and drained

1 cup chopped onions

1 cup chopped carrots

1 stalk celery, finely chopped

½ cup pearled barley

2 Tablespoons extra-virgin olive oil

1 Tablespoon crushed garlic

1 teaspoon thyme

Salt and pepper

1. Place the water and beans in a large soup pot or Dutch oven, and bring to a boil. Add the remaining ingredients, except the salt and pepper.

2. Return to a boil, reduce the heat to medium, cover, and simmer until the barley and beans are tender and the broth is creamy, about 1½ to 2 hours. Season with salt and pepper. Serve hot.

Per cup: Calories 159,
Protein 5 g, Fat 2 g,
Carbohydrates 26 g

CURRIED YELLOW SPLIT PEA SOUP

Yield: about 1½ quarts

Hot and spicy, this soup is both soothing and energizing. Like most bean soups, it's even better the next day, when the flavors have mingled overnight.

1. Place the water and split peas in a large soup pot or Dutch oven, and bring to a boil. Boil uncovered for 2 minutes. Remove from the heat, cover, and let stand for 1 hour.

2. About 10 minutes before the peas are finished standing, heat the oil in a large skillet. Add the onion, carrots, and garlic, and sauté for 10 minutes. Stir in the curry powder, and remove from the heat.

3. Stir the vegetables into the peas, and bring to a boil. Reduce the heat to medium, cover, and simmer for 1 hour. Add the dill and continue to cook, stirring occasionally, for at least 60 minutes longer, or until the peas have practically disintegrated. Season with salt. Serve hot.

6 cups water

1½ cups yellow split peas, rinsed and drained

2 Tablespoons extra-virgin olive oil

1 large onion, chopped

1 cup chopped carrots

½ teaspoon crushed garlic

1½ Tablespoons curry powder

2 teaspoons dill

Salt

***Tip:** If leftover soup becomes too thick, thin it with a little extra water, or serve like a stew over rice or bulgur.*

Per cup: Calories 214, Protein 10 g, Fat 5 g, Carbohydrates 32 g

CREAM OF CAULIFLOWER & LIMA BEAN SOUP

Yield: about 2 quarts

This is a creamy blended soup, with a few whole lima beans added for extra bite. Use only Fordhook lima beans, which are large, sweet, and meaty.

16-ounce package frozen Fordhook lima beans

1 Tablespoon extra-virgin olive oil

1½ cups chopped onions

2 teaspoons whole caraway seeds, or 1½ teaspoons ground caraway

1 teaspoon crushed garlic

1 medium cauliflower, cut into small florets

5 cups water

Salt and pepper

Minced fresh parsley (optional)

1. Cook the lima beans according to the package directions. Drain and divide in half.

2. Heat the oil in a large soup pot or Dutch oven over medium-high. Add the onions, caraway seeds, and garlic, and cook, stirring often, until the onions are soft, about 10 to 15 minutes.

3. Add the cauliflower and water, and bring to a boil. Reduce the heat to medium, cover, and simmer until the cauliflower is very tender, about 10 to 12 minutes.

4. In a blender, purée the soup in batches along with half the lima beans. Return the blended soup to the soup pot, and stir in the remaining lima beans.

5. Season with salt and pepper. Warm over medium-low until the beans are heated through, and the soup is hot. Garnish with chopped parsley, if desired.

Per cup: Calories 91,
Protein 4 g, Fat 1 g,
Carbohydrates 15 g

CREAM OF BROCCOLI CHOWDER

Yield: about 1 quart

*T*here are many good cream of broccoli soup recipes, but this one is truly different and special.

1. Combine the broccoli, water, onion, carrot, and garlic in a soup pot or Dutch oven, and bring to a boil. Reduce the heat, cover, and steam until very tender. Add a little more water during cooking, if necessary, to keep the vegetables from sticking. Mash well with a potato masher or sturdy fork. The vegetables will still be somewhat chunky.

2. While the vegetables are cooking, combine the flour and oil in a large saucepan, and cook for about 2 minutes. Remove the pan from the heat, and gradually whisk in the hot milk. Whisk vigorously, and scrape the bottom and sides of the pan to incorporate all of the oil and flour mixture and prevent lumps. Stir in the seasonings and simmer several minutes until thickened, whisking occasionally. Stir into the mashed vegetables, and simmer for a few minutes. Remove the bay leaf before serving.

3 cups finely chopped broccoli

1 cup water

1 medium onion, diced

1 medium carrot, chopped

½ teaspoon crushed garlic

¼ cup whole grain flour (whole wheat, barley, rye, or spelt)

2 Tablespoons extra-virgin olive oil

3 cups hot nondairy milk

1 bay leaf

¼ teaspoon turmeric

Large pinch *each*: nutmeg, ground ginger, salt, and pepper

Per cup: Calories 200, Protein 7 g, Fat 10 g, Carbohydrates 20 g

Purée of Parsnips & Leeks

Yield: 1½ quarts

*T*he delicate sweet taste of parsnips gets zapped with the oniony flavor of leeks and the peppery bite of ginger in this light and creamy soup.

❧

1 Tablespoon extra-virgin olive oil

1 cup sliced leeks

1 teaspoon ground ginger

4 cups water

1½ pounds parsnips, peeled and coarsely chopped

1 cup hot nondairy milk

Salt

Paprika

1. Heat the oil in a large soup pot or Dutch oven over medium-high. When the oil is hot, add the leeks, and sauté for 5 minutes. Add the ginger and cook for 1 minute, stirring constantly. Add the water and parsnips and bring to a boil. Reduce the heat to low, cover, and simmer, stirring occasionally, until the parsnips are very tender, about 25 to 30 minutes.

2. Purée the soup in batches in a blender. Return the blended soup to the soup pot, and stir in the hot milk. Warm the soup, stirring constantly, until it is just heated through, about 5 minutes. Season with salt. Garnish each serving with a light dusting of paprika.

Tip: Rinse leeks thoroughly to remove the sandy grit and dirt. The easiest way to do this is to slice halfway through each bulb lengthwise, and separate the leaves gently so the inner sections of the leek are exposed and can be readily cleaned.

Per cup: Calories 135, Protein 2 g, Fat 3 g, Carbohydrates 24 g

SPEEDY CORN SOUP

Yield: about 1½ quarts

*B*read is the secret thickening ingredient in this simple, lightning-fast soup.

1. Process all the ingredients, except the water, in a blender until the corn is well puréed.

2. Transfer to a large soup pot or Dutch oven. Add water, as needed, to thin to the desired consistency. Warm gently over medium heat until hot. Do not boil.

2 cups corn kernels (see Tip below)

1½ cups plain nondairy milk

2 slices whole grain bread, torn (remove crusts, if desired)

¼ cup chopped onions

1 Tablespoon extra-virgin olive oil

1 teaspoon salt

Pepper

1 to 1½ cups water, as needed

Tip: *Use fresh corn kernels, drained canned corn, or thawed and drained frozen corn.*

Per cup: Calories 103, Protein 3 g, Fat 3 g, Carbohydrates 15 g

STEWED WINTER VEGETABLES

Yield: 4 to 6 servings

*T*his *is the vegetarian answer to chicken soup! It's soothing, healing, and satisfying. The flavor is sweet and mild, and the texture is thick and juicy. Serve it with plenty of whole grain bread to dip into the delicious broth.*

❦

6 to 8 cups winter vegetables, peeled and cut into equal-size chunks (see Tips below)

1 large onion, cut into wedges

6 to 8 cloves garlic (whole, halved, sliced, or coarsely chopped)

Water, as needed

2 cups torn or chopped greens, or ½ to 1 cup chopped fresh parsley (see Tips below)

1 Tablespoon extra-virgin olive oil (optional)

Salt

1. Place the vegetables, onion, and garlic in a large soup pot or Dutch oven. Add enough water to more than cover the vegetables. The more water you use, the more broth you will have. However, do not fill the saucepan more than two-thirds full with vegetables and water. This will help to prevent the contents from boiling over as the soup cooks.

2 Bring to a boil, reduce the heat to medium-low, cover, and simmer for 30 minutes. Stir in the greens or parsley, cover, and continue to simmer until everything is very tender and the vegetables are starting to break apart, about 10 to 15 minutes. Stir in the olive oil, if using, and season with salt.

Tips: For the winter vegetables, choose a mix of yams, rutabaga, turnips, parsnips, potatoes, and carrots.

For the greens, choose from kale, collard greens, turnip greens, or mustard greens.

To prevent the yams from discoloring after they have been peeled and chunked, place them in a bowl of water to which a little lemon juice has been added. When the remaining vegetables have been prepared, place the yams in a colander, and rinse off the lemon water thoroughly before proceeding with the recipe.

Per serving: Calories 216, Protein 3 g, Fat 0 g, Carbohydrates 49 g

Blender Gazpacho

Yield: 1 quart

A *warm weather delight, this "liquefied salad" is light and spicy.*

1. Combine all the ingredients in a blender. Pulse the blender briefly, just until everything is well combined but the vegetables are still somewhat chunky.

2. Transfer to a covered storage container, and chill for several hours before serving. Serve cold. Garnish, if desired.

2 cups canned crushed tomatoes

1½ cups chunked English cucumber

1 cup tomato juice

1 small red or yellow bell pepper, chopped

½ cup chopped red onions

3 Tablespoons fresh lemon juice

3 Tablespoons red wine vinegar

1 Tablespoon organic flax oil or extra-virgin olive oil

½ teaspoon crushed garlic

¼ teaspoon pepper

Several drops bottled hot sauce

Optional garnishes: *Tofu Sour Cream, p. 129, chopped fresh cilantro*

Per cup: Calories 87, Protein 2 g, Fat 2 g, Carbohydrates 12 g

Fresh Tomato Panade (Bread & Tomato Soup)

Yield: 4 servings

A panade is a soup that is thickened with bread. Slightly stale bread is ideal, and this is a great way to use it up. Use the best tasting bread you have available, as it will add a gorgeous flavor to your soup. It's also worth the effort to find extra juicy, red ripe tomatoes to infuse your soup with outstanding taste and a rich texture.

❦

1 Tablespoon extra-virgin olive oil

1 small onion, diced

½ teaspoon crushed garlic

4 ripe tomatoes, coarsely chopped

2 Tablespoons tomato paste

Pinch of crushed red pepper flakes

2½ cups vegetable stock or water

1½ cups whole grain bread cubes, firmly packed

¼ cup torn fresh basil leaves, or 1 teaspoon dried basil

Salt and pepper

1. Heat the oil in a soup pot or Dutch oven over medium-high. Add the onion and garlic, reduce the heat to medium, and sauté until the onion is tender and golden brown, about 15 minutes.

2. Add the tomatoes, tomato paste, and red pepper flakes, stirring until the tomato paste is well incorporated. Raise the heat to bring the mixture up to a simmer, then simmer uncovered for 20 minutes, stirring occasionally. Adjust the heat as necessary to keep the tomatoes from scorching.

3. After 20 minutes, add the stock or water, bread cubes, and basil. Bring to a boil, reduce the heat, and simmer uncovered 10 to 15 minutes, stirring occasionally and mashing the bread into the soup with the back of a wooden spoon. Take care that the bread doesn't scorch on the bottom of the saucepan. Season with salt and pepper. Serve hot, warm, or cold.

Per serving: Calories 121,
Protein 3 g, Fat 5 g,
Carbohydrates 17 g

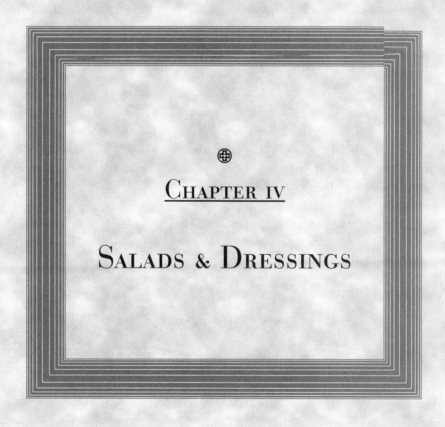

CHAPTER IV

SALADS & DRESSINGS

UNRULY TABOULI

Yield: 4 to 6 servings

*A*though this Middle Eastern grain salad doesn't take much time or effort to prepare, it must marinate in the refrigerator for several hours to properly soften the bulgur. It's worth the wait, however, as the long marinating time ensures each grain is infused with eye-popping flavor.

When options are added, this tabouli is transformed from an auxiliary role to the main attraction. Just add a light soup and warm pita bread to round out your meal.

Salad mix:

1 cup bulgur

1 teaspoon salt

1½ cups boiling water

¼ cup fresh lemon juice

2 Tablespoons extra-virgin olive oil

2 Tablespoons organic flax oil

1 cup finely chopped parsley, firmly packed

4 scallions, thinly sliced

1½ teaspoons dried spearmint

½ teaspoon crushed garlic

Unruly options:

1 cup cooked garbanzo beans

1 cup diced English cucumber

½ to 1 cup additional chopped parsley

1 ripe tomato, diced

½ cup sliced red radishes

½ cup finely minced bell pepper

½ cup grated carrot

1. Place the bulgur in a heat-proof bowl. Dissolve the salt in the boiling water, and pour over the bulgur. Mix well, cover, and let sit for 30 minutes.

2. Combine the lemon juice, olive oil, and flax oil, and add to the bulgur.

3. Stir in the parsley, scallions, spearmint, and garlic, and mix well. Cover tightly and marinate the salad in the refrigerator for 4 to 12 hours. If desired, toss or top with your choice of optional additions shortly before serving.

Per serving: Calories 240,
Protein 5 g, Fat 10 g,
Carbohydrates 30 g

Warm Salad Niçoise

Yield: 4 to 6 servings

Traditionally, one of the main components of salad niçoise is tuna fish. In this modified version, the tuna fish has been replaced with garbanzo beans, and the large quantity of olive oil typically called for has been greatly reduced. Nevertheless, this rendition retains all the flavor for which salad niçoise is renowned.

1. To make the dressing, whisk together the olive oil, lemon juice, vinegar, mustard, garlic, sugar, herbs, and salt in small bowl. Set aside.

2. Steam the potatoes and green beans until tender. Place in a large bowl with the garbanzo beans, tomato wedges, and onions. Drizzle the dressing over the vegetables and beans. Top with the nori flakes, and toss gently to mix.

3. Divide the salad greens among 4 to 6 salad plates. Top with the vegetable and bean mixture, and serve.

Tip: *Green nori flakes are available in the macrobiotic section of natural food stores.*

Niçoise Dressing:
- 1½ Tablespoons extra-virgin olive oil
- 2 Tablespoons fresh lemon juice
- 1 Tablespoon red wine vinegar
- 1 teaspoon Dijon mustard
- ½ teaspoon crushed garlic
- ½ teaspoon sugar
- ¼ teaspoon dried basil
- ¼ teaspoon dried oregano
- ¼ teaspoon salt

Salad mix:
- 3 small to medium red-skin potatoes, cut into bite-size chunks
- 2 cups fresh green beans, trimmed and cut into 1- to 2-inch pieces
- 1¾ cups cooked garbanzo beans, rinsed and drained
- 2 tomatoes, each cut in 8 wedges
- ¼ cup minced red onions
- 2 to 4 Tablespoons green nori flakes
- 4 cups mixed salad greens, torn

Per serving: Calories 233,
Protein 6 g, Fat 5 g,
Carbohydrates 38 g

67

Wilted Spinach Salad with Raspberry Vinaigrette

Yield: 4 servings

*T*his scrumptious salad is effortless to prepare, making it perfect for everyday service, but its elegant presentation also makes it ideal for company.

❦

Salad mix:

6 cups fresh spinach leaves, lightly packed

1 cup thinly sliced mushrooms

2 very thin slices red onion, cut in half and separated into crescents

Raspberry Vinaigrette:

1½ Tablespoons extra-virgin olive oil

1 teaspoon crushed garlic

2 Tablespoons seedless raspberry jelly

2 Tablespoons red wine vinegar

Pinch of salt and pepper

¼ cup sunflower seeds or coarsely chopped walnuts, lightly pan toasted

Per serving: Calories 151, Protein 4 g, Fat 8 g, Carbohydrates 12 g

1. Remove the stems of the spinach, and rinse the leaves well. Dry thoroughly either by patting with a clean kitchen towel or spinning in a salad spinner. Tear into large pieces and place in a large bowl along with the mushrooms and onion.

2. To make the dressing, heat the oil in a small skillet or saucepan. Add the garlic and stir-fry for 30 seconds. Add the raspberry jelly, vinegar, salt, and pepper. Heat just until the jelly is melted and bubbly. Remove from the heat.

3. Pour the warm dressing over the spinach leaves, mushrooms, and onion. Toss until everything is evenly coated. Top each serving with a tablespoon of the seeds or nuts. Serve at once.

Tip: To pan toast the sunflower seeds or walnuts, lightly roast them in a dry skillet over medium heat, stirring often, until fragrant and golden brown.

Italian Bean & Tomato Salad

Yield: 2 to 4 servings

*W*hen served with warm, crusty Italian bread, this hearty salad makes a complete summer meal.

1. Combine the lettuce, beans, tomatoes, and carrot in a large bowl.
2. Whisk together the dressing ingredients in a separate small bowl. Pour over the salad and toss gently. Serve at room temperature or chilled.

Salad mix:

3 cups torn romaine or leaf lettuce, lightly packed

1½ cups cooked white beans, rinsed and drained

6 cherry tomatoes, quartered

1 large carrot, shredded

Soy Vinaigrette:

2 Tablespoons natural soy sauce

2 Tablespoons balsamic vinegar

1 Tablespoon extra-virgin olive oil

1 Tablespoon organic flax oil

½ teaspoon dried basil

Pinch of salt and pepper

Per serving: Calories 218, Protein 8 g, Fat 8 g, Carbohydrates 25 g

BLACK BEAN & ROASTED RED PEPPER SALAD

Yield: 4 to 6 servings

Serve this salad chilled for a hot weather lunch or dinner. Or serve it at room temperature for a hearty autumn or winter meal. With its light and zesty vinaigrette, this dish is a great company pleaser.

Salad mix:

3 cups cooked black beans, rinsed and drained

1 cup chopped roasted red bell peppers (see Tip below)

½ cup diced red onions

¼ cup minced fresh parsley

2 stalks celery, finely diced

Citrus Vinaigrette:

2 tablespoons extra-virgin olive oil

1½ Tablespoons fresh lemon juice

1½ Tablespoons balsamic vinegar

1 Tablespoon frozen orange juice concentrate, thawed

2 teaspoons natural soy sauce

1 teaspoon sugar

½ teaspoon crushed garlic

Pinch of salt

1. Combine the salad mix ingredients in a large bowl.

2. In a separate small bowl, whisk together the dressing ingredients. Pour over the salad and toss gently. Serve at room temperature or chilled.

Tip: Roasted red bell peppers are available in cans or jars at supermarkets and Italian grocery stores.

Per serving: Calories 208,
Protein 8 g, Fat 6 g,
Carbohydrates 30 g

FATOOSH

Yield: 4 servings

*T*his *special Syrian-style vegetable salad includes pieces of toasted pita triangles. What an ingenious way to use up slightly stale bread!*

1. Slice the pita bread into 8 triangles. Separate each triangle into 2 thin triangles to make 16 pieces in all. Place on a dry baking sheet, and toast briefly under the broiler, just until crisp and lightly brown. Watch closely so the bread does not burn; this will only take a few minutes. Break the triangles into large pieces, and set aside.

2. Combine the remaining salad ingredients in a large bowl. In a separate small bowl, whisk together the dressing ingredients until well blended. Pour over the salad and toss gently. Add the toasted pita pieces, and toss once more. Serve at once.

Salad mix:

1 whole wheat pita bread

2 cups finely torn romaine lettuce leaves, lightly packed

2 ripe tomatoes, chopped

1 small cucumber, chopped

2 scallions, thinly sliced

2 Tablespoons minced fresh parsley

½ to 1 teaspoon dried spearmint or oregano

Lemon-Garlic Dressing:

2 Tablespoons fresh lemon juice

1 Tablespoon extra-virgin olive oil

1 Tablespoon organic flax oil

½ teaspoon crushed garlic

Pinch of salt and pepper

Per serving: Calories 125, Protein 2 g, Fat 7 g, Carbohydrates 12 g

71

Brussels Sprouts Salad

Yield: 4 servings

*T*his makes a particularly delicious side dish for veggie burgers, and it's always welcome at picnics and barbecues.

❧

1 pound fresh brussels sprouts, scrubbed and trimmed

Dijon Vinaigrette:

3 Tablespoons red wine vinegar

2 Tablespoons extra-virgin olive oil

1 Tablespoon organic flax oil

1 Tablespoon Dijon mustard

2 teaspoons sugar

1 ripe tomato, chopped

½ cup finely chopped red onions

Salt and pepper

1. Cut the brussels sprouts in half if they are small, or in quarters if they are large. Steam until bright green and very tender. Set aside to cool.

2. In a large bowl, whisk together the vinaigrette ingredients until well blended. Add the brussels sprouts and toss until evenly coated. Add the tomato, onions, salt, and pepper. Toss gently but thoroughly. Serve at once, or marinate in the refrigerator for several hours to allow the flavors to blend.

Per serving: Calories 157,
Protein 2 g, Fat 10 g,
Carbohydrates 13 g

72

Tomato-Garlic Dressing

Yield: about ¼ cup

Tangy and rich tasting, this dressing coats lettuce leaves with a burst of flavor instead of fat.

Combine all the ingredients in a small measuring cup or bowl, and whisk together until blended.

2 Tablespoons ketchup

2 Tablespoons brown rice vinegar or balsamic vinegar

1 teaspoon Dijon mustard

¼ teaspoon crushed garlic

Per 2 tablespoons: Calories 21,
Protein 0 g, Fat 0 g,
Carbohydrates 5 g

Classic Ranch Dressing

Yield: about ¾ cup

All the rich taste and allure of creamy ranch dressing, with a fraction of the calories and none of the objectionable dairy fat.

Combine all the ingredients in a blender or food processor, and process until smooth and creamy.

¾ cup silken tofu, crumbled

2 Tablespoons extra-virgin olive oil

1 Tablespoon umeboshi plum vinegar

1 Tablespoon fresh lemon juice

1 Tablespoon water

½ teaspoon tarragon

¼ teaspoon dill

¼ teaspoon crushed garlic

Pinch of dry mustard

Per 2 tablespoons: Calories 56,
Protein 1 g, Fat 5 g,
Carbohydrates 1 g

73

Flax & Olive Vinaigrette

Yield: a scant ⅔ cup

*T*his tart and tangy dressing is a delicious way to add the healthful benefits of flax and olive oil to your diet.

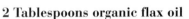

2 Tablespoons organic flax oil

2 Tablespoons extra-virgin olive oil

1½ Tablespoons Dijon mustard

1½ Tablespoons umeboshi vinegar

1½ Tablespoons brown rice vinegar

1½ Tablespoons fresh lemon juice

Pinch of sugar

Combine all the ingredients in a small measuring cup or bowl, and whisk together until blended.

Per 2 tablespoons: Calories 105, Protein 0 g, Fat 11 g, Carbohydrates 1 g

Thousand Island Dressing

Yield: about ¾ cup

*T*housand Island dressing used to mean *"a thousand calories and fat grams." No longer! Indulge your senses with this thick and luxurious, but healthful, low-fat temptation.*

Combine all the ingredients in a blender or food processor fitted with a metal blade, and process until creamy.

½ cup silken tofu, crumbled

2 Tablespoons ketchup

1½ Tablespoons pickle relish, lightly drained

1 Tablespoon extra-virgin olive oil

1 Tablespoon fresh lemon juice

1 Tablespoon chopped onions, or ½ teaspoon onion powder

Pinch of salt

Per 2 tablespoons: Calories 41,
Protein 1 g, Fat 3 g,
Carbohydrates 4 g

SWEET 'N SMOKY VINAIGRETTE

Yield: about 1 cup

An unusual combination of ingredients makes for a unique but compelling flavor that is sure to tantalize.

❦

¼ cup ketchup

¼ cup extra-virgin olive oil

¼ cup orange juice

¼ cup brown rice vinegar

2 Tablespoons sugar

½ teaspoon crushed garlic

¼ teaspoon salt

¼ teaspoon pepper

Several drops liquid hickory
   smoke

Combine all the ingredients in a blender, and process several minutes until smooth and well blended. Alternatively, combine all the ingredients in a small bowl, and vigorously whisk together until emulsified and smooth.

Per 2 tablespoons: Calories 84,
Protein 0 g, Fat 7 g,
Carbohydrates 7 g

Miso Master Dressing

Yield: about ¾ cup

*S*weet white miso blended with simple seasonings creates an amazingly zesty and delicious dressing.

Combine all the ingredients in a blender or food processor, and process until smooth.

3 Tablespoons sweet white miso

2 Tablespoons extra-virgin olive oil

2 Tablespoons organic flax oil

2 Tablespoons water

2 Tablespoons brown rice vinegar

2 Tablespoons brown rice syrup

2 Tablespoons chopped onions

1 teaspoon Dijon mustard

Per 2 tablespoons: Calories 119, Protein 1 g, Fat 8 g, Carbohydrates 8 g

POWER DRESSING

Yield: about ⅓ cup

*T**his healthful mix of flax oil, olive oil, and nutritional yeast will put zip in your salad and zing in your stride.*

2 Tablespoons nutritional
yeast flakes

2 Tablespoons extra-virgin
olive oil

1 Tablespoon organic flax oil

1 Tablespoon fresh lemon
juice

1 Tablespoon water

½ teaspoon natural soy sauce

Combine all the ingredients in a small bowl, and whisk together until well combined.

Per tablespoon: Calories 83,
Protein 2 g, Fat 8 g,
Carbohydrates 2 g

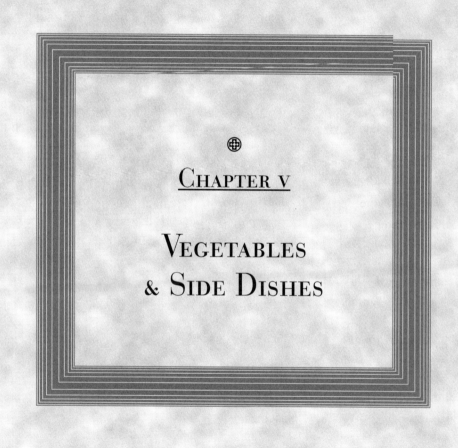

⊕

Chapter V

Vegetables
& Side Dishes

Broccoli or Asparagus with No-Cook Hollandaise Sauce

Yield: 4 to 6 servings

*H*ollandaise sauce makes all vegetables take notice. This egg- and butter-free version is simple to prepare. Try it on asparagus, for a classic dish, or carrots or cauliflower. Your taste buds will applaud you, and your heart will thank you.

❦

4 to 6 cups broccoli florets, or 2 pounds trimmed asparagus spears

No-Cook Hollandaise Sauce:

1 cup silken tofu, crumbled

2 Tablespoons water

1 Tablespoon extra-virgin olive oil

1 Tablespoon organic flax oil

1 Tablespoon fresh lemon juice

1 Tablespoon nutritional yeast flakes

1 Tablespoon tahini

1 teaspoon prepared yellow mustard

½ teaspoon tarragon

1. Steam the broccoli or asparagus until bright green and tender-crisp. Serve with the sauce on the side.

2. To prepare No-Cook Hollandaise Sauce, combine all the ingredients in a blender or food processor fitted with a metal blade, and process until creamy; then chill. Stir before serving. This makes about 1 cup of sauce.

Per serving: Calories 121,
Protein 5 g, Fat 8 g,
Carbohydrates 7 g

STEAK FRIES

Yield: 2 to 4 servings

*T*hick, oven-baked french fried are low in fat but resonate with fabulous flavor.

❧

1. Preheat the oven to 450°F. Oil a large baking sheet, or line it with parchment paper for easy clean up, and set aside.

2. Scrub the potatoes well and remove any eyes and discolored areas. Peel, if desired, and cut into wedges or french fry shapes. Place in a large bowl, sprinkle with oil, and toss to coat evenly. Sprinkle with the seasonings and toss again so all the pieces are evenly coated.

3. Arrange in a single layer on the prepared baking sheet. Bake until golden brown and fork tender, about 30 minutes. For more even browning, turn over once midway in the cooking cycle.

2 large russet potatoes

1 Tablespoon extra-virgin olive oil

1 teaspoon paprika

¼ teaspoon salt

Dash *each*: pepper, garlic powder, and turmeric

Tips: *If you like your fries a little spicier, omit the paprika and instead use ½ teaspoon curry powder, hot Hungarian paprika, or chili powder.*

Leftover baked or steamed potatoes can also be oven fried. Cut them into chunks, and prepare and bake them as directed above. Even though they are already cooked, they will become golden brown, crusty, and even more tender when prepared in this simple fashion.

Per serving: Calories 156, Protein 2 g, Fat 4 g, Carbohydrates 27 g

Easy Baked Beans

Yield: 2 to 4 servings

A *time-honored classic made simple.*

❧

1 Tablespoon extra-virgin
olive oil

1 large onion, finely chopped

1 teaspoon crushed garlic

¼ cup tomato paste

2 Tablespoons natural soy
sauce

1 to 2 Tablespoons light
molasses or pure maple
syrup

1 teaspoon prepared yellow
mustard

1¾ cups cooked navy beans,
rinsed and drained

1. Preheat the oven to 350°F. Lightly oil a 1-quart casserole dish, or mist it with nonstick cooking spray, and set aside.

2. Heat the oil in a medium skillet over medium-high. When hot, add the onion and garlic, and sauté until the onion is well browned and very tender.

3. Meanwhile, combine the tomato paste, soy sauce, molasses or maple syrup, and mustard in a large bowl. Mix well to form a smooth, thick sauce. Add the beans and mix gently.

4. Stir the cooked onion into the beans. Spoon into the prepared casserole dish. Cover tightly and bake for 30 minutes.

Per serving: Calories 272,
Protein 10 g, Fat 6 g,
Carbohydrates 46 g

Variation: Substitute cooked lima beans, great Northern beans, or pinto beans for the navy beans.

Oven-Roasted Parsnip Fries

Yield: 2 to 4 servings

Roasting brings out the natural sweetness of parsnips, making a heavenly side dish for this much under-appreciated vegetable.

1. Preheat the oven to 450°F. Oil a large baking sheet, or line it with parchment paper for easy clean up, and set aside.

2. Peel and trim the parsnips, and cut them into french fry shapes or ¼-inch-thick slices cut on a diagonal. Place in a large bowl, sprinkle with the oil, and toss to coat evenly. Sprinkle on the seasonings, and toss again so all the pieces are evenly coated.

3. Arrange in a single layer on the prepared baking sheet. Bake until golden brown and fork-tender, about 30 to 40 minutes. Stir or turn over once midway in the cooking cycle.

1 pound parsnips

1 Tablespoon extra-virgin olive oil

½ teaspoon paprika

¼ teaspoon salt

Dash of turmeric

Tip: This recipe is easily doubled, and leftovers make a great snack straight from the refrigerator.

Per serving: Calories 162, Protein 1 g, Fat 4 g, Carbohydrates 28 g

83

Red Cabbage & Apples

Yield: 4 servings

A perennial palate pleaser, this sweet and sour cabbage recipe always conjures up fond memories.

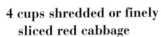

4 cups shredded or finely sliced red cabbage

1 large tart apple, peeled and diced

½ cup chopped onions

¼ cup frozen apple juice concentrate, thawed

2 Tablespoons water

1 teaspoon caraway seeds

2 Tablespoons red wine vinegar

1. Combine the cabbage, apple, onions, juice concentrate, water, and caraway seeds in a large saucepan. Bring to a boil, reduce the heat to medium-low, cover, and simmer until the cabbage is tender, about 8 to 12 minutes.

2. Stir in the vinegar, and toss to coat the cabbage thoroughly. Serve hot or warm, using a slotted spoon.

Per serving: Calories 77,
Protein 1 g, Fat 0 g,
Carbohydrates 18 g

GREENS & GARLIC

Yield: 4 servings

*T*his is an absolutely spectacular way to serve greens! Don't be intimidated by the large quantity of garlic. Thinly sliced garlic is surprisingly mild, because very little of its pungent oil is released. Garlic has been attributed with wonderful medicinal properties, so you can never eat too much.

1. Heat the oil in a very large saucepan or Dutch oven. When hot, add the garlic and cook for 30 seconds. Add the greens, toss to coat with the oil, and stir-fry until slightly wilted, about 2 to 5 minutes.

2. Pour in just enough water to cover the bottom of the pan, and bring to a boil. Reduce the heat slightly, cover, and steam, stirring occasionally, for 12 to 18 minutes, or until the greens are tender. There should be very little liquid left in the saucepan. If there is liquid, uncover and simmer briefly until it cooks off.

3. Stir in the seasoning options of your choice. Serve hot or warm.

Vegetable mix:

2 Tablespoons extra-virgin olive oil

6 to 8 cloves garlic, very thinly sliced

8 cups greens, torn or chopped into small pieces (see Tip below)

¼ to ½ cup water, as needed

Seasoning options:

Several drops bottled hot sauce

Fresh lemon juice

Salt

Tip: For the greens, use collards, kale, mustard greens, turnip greens or beet greens, or a mixture of two or more.

Per serving: Calories 135, Protein 3 g, Fat 7 g, Carbohydrates 14 g

SLOW-BAKED TOMATOES

Yield: 4 servings

*M*mmm . . . *sweet, simple, and savory. Although nothing beats a fresh ripe tomato in the buff, slow-baked tomatoes are sure a close runner-up.*

❧

4 large, firm ripe tomatoes

2 Tablespoons extra-virgin olive oil

1 to 2 teaspoons crushed garlic

3 Tablespoons chopped fresh basil or parsley (optional)

Salt

Per serving: Calories 90, Protein 1 g, Fat 7 g, Carbohydrates 6 g

1. Preheat the oven to 325°F. Core the tomatoes and slice off a thin portion of the tops. Discard the core and tops, or save them to make stock. Place the tomatoes on a baking sheet, cut side up. Whisk together the olive oil and garlic, and drizzle generously over the tomatoes.

2. Bake for 1 hour, basting occasionally. Just before serving, sprinkle with the fresh herbs, if using, and salt. Serve hot or at room temperature.

CRUSTY CARROT STICKS

Yield: 2 to 4 servings

*O*ne of the easiest and most delicious ways to serve nutritious, sweet carrots.

1 pound carrots

1 Tablespoon organic flax oil or extra-virgin olive oil

3 Tablespoons nutritional yeast flakes

½ teaspoon seasoned salt (such as Spike)

Per serving: Calories 131, Protein 4 g, Fat 4 g, Carbohydrates 18 g

Peel and trim the carrots, and cut them into sticks about ½ inch thick by 3 inches long. Steam until tender. Transfer to a large bowl. Sprinkle with the oil and toss gently. Sprinkle with the remaining ingredients, and toss again until the seasonings are evenly distributed.

STEAMED SWEETS

Yield: 2 to 4 servings

Quicker than baking, steamed sweet potatoes are soft, creamy, and satisfying. Select long, thin sweet potatoes for the best and fastest results. My favorites are organic jewel and garnet yams, which have a beautiful reddish-purple skin and richly colored flesh

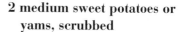

Quarter the sweet potatoes by cutting them in half widthwise and again lengthwise. Steam until fork tender. Serve as is or scoop out of the skin. The flesh can be mashed with a fork, if desired. Drizzle with the oils. Season with a pinch of salt and a little soy sauce.

2 medium sweet potatoes or yams, scrubbed

2 teaspoons extra-virgin olive oil

2 teaspoons organic flax oil

Pinch of salt

Natural soy sauce

Tip: *This recipe is easily doubled. Just stack the sweet potatoes in layers in the steamer.*

Per serving: Calories 210, Protein 2 g, Fat 6 g, Carbohydrates 37 g

Steamed or Baked Winter Squash

Yield: 2 to 4 servings

Although hard-shell squash is considered a cold weather staple, you can make it year-round if you like.

1 medium winter squash

2 Tablespoons pure maple syrup

1 Tablespoon organic flax oil

1 Tablespoon natural soy sauce

1. Cut the squash in half from stem to tip, and scoop out the seeds with a spoon. Keep in halves or cut into quarters. Steam until tender. Alternatively, place the squash cut side down in a pan with ¼-inch of water, and bake at 350°F until fork tender, about 30 to 60 minutes. The time it takes to reach tenderness will vary depending on the type, age, and thickness of the squash. Serve in the shell or scoop out into a bowl or onto a plate.

2. Whisk together the maple syrup, flax oil, and soy sauce. Drizzle over the cooked squash.

Per serving: Calories 181,
Protein 3 g, Fat 6 g,
Carbohydrates 30 g

Tip: *Use any winter squash that's in season, such as butternut, acorn, turban, or kabocha.*

Lemon Parslied New Potatoes

Yield: 4 servings

A simple sauce complements the tender texture of creamy new potatoes.

Steam the potatoes until tender. In a large bowl, whisk together the remaining ingredients, except the parsley, salt, and pepper. Add the hot potatoes, and toss gently. Add the parsley, and toss gently again. Season with salt and pepper.

1 pound small new potatoes, scrubbed and halved or quartered

1 Tablespoon fresh lemon juice

2 teaspoons extra-virgin olive oil

2 teaspoons organic flax oil

1 teaspoon Dijon mustard

½ teaspoon crushed garlic

2 Tablespoons minced fresh parsley

Salt and pepper

Per serving: Calories 141,
Protein 1 g, Fat 5 g,
Carbohydrates 23 g

GARLIC INFUSED SMASHED POTATOES

Yield: 2 to 3 servings

This quick and easy standard is incredibly low in fat and utterly delicious.

❧

Potato mix:

2 large russet potatoes, peeled and cubed

2 to 4 Tablespoons potato cooking water or plain nondairy milk, as needed

Garlic powder or crushed garlic

Salt and pepper

Seasoning options:

1 to 2 Tablespoons nutritional yeast flakes

1 Tablespoon organic flax oil or extra-virgin olive oil

Thinly sliced scallions or chives

Minced fresh parsley, cilantro, or basil

Dried basil or dill

Per serving: Calories 139, Protein 2 g, Fat 0 g, Carbohydrates 33 g

1. Fill a 4½-quart saucepan or Dutch oven halfway with water. Add the potatoes and bring to a boil. Reduce the heat to medium, cover, and cook until the potatoes are tender.

2. Transfer the potatoes from the saucepan to a large bowl using a slotted spoon. Mash the potatoes with a potato masher, electric hand beater, or sturdy fork. Add a little cooking water or nondairy milk, 1 tablespoon at a time, if the potatoes seem dry. Season with garlic, salt, pepper, and any of the options you like.

Tips: If you aren't serving the potatoes immediately, they may be kept hot for about 30 minutes in a double boiler.

If you are using flax oil, do not add it until just before serving, because flax oil should not be heated.

For a more delicate and different taste, try mixing in other mashed, cooked vegetables, such as carrots, parsnips, or peeled winter squash. To avoid washing an additional pot, cook these vegetables right along with the potatoes.

CHAPTER VI

PLAIN & FANCY
GRAINS

Perfectly Cooked Basic Brown Rice

Yield: 3 to 4 servings

*T*his recipe is a standard you're bound to use often. Brown rice is the perfect side dish for so many great foods. You can also chill it and use it as the basis for a grain salad, or add it to soups and casseroles.

2 cups water

1 Tablespoon canola oil or extra-virgin olive oil (optional)

½ teaspoon salt

1 cup brown rice, rinsed and drained

Pressure cooker method: Place the water, oil, if using, and salt in a 3½-quart or larger pressure cooker, and bring to a boil. Stir in the rice, lock the lid in place, and bring up to high pressure over high heat. Reduce the heat just enough to maintain high pressure, and cook for 40 minutes.

2. Remove from the heat and let the pressure come down naturally for 10 minutes to complete the cooking. Fluff and serve.

Standard stovetop method: Place the water, rice, oil, if using, and salt in a heavy saucepan. Bring to a boil. Immediately reduce the heat to very low, and cover the pot with a tight-fitting lid. If your pot has a loose lid, you may need to add ¼ cup or more additional water. Cook undisturbed for 1 hour. Do not peek inside the pot!

2. Remove from the heat, and stir up the grain so the drier kernels on top are mixed with the wetter ones on the bottom. Place a clean tea towel over the pot. Replace the lid snugly over the towel, and let sit for 5 minutes. The towel will absorb any excess moisture. Fluff again and serve.

Tips: *For the most delicious, tender, and digestible rice, soak the rice in the 2 cups water for 6 to 8 hours prior to cooking. Do not drain. To retain all the nutrients, always use the same water for cooking as for soaking. To cook, add the remaining ingredients, and follow the directions for either method above.*

Per serving: Calories 197, Protein 4 g, Fat 0 g, Carbohydrates 43 g

FANCY RICE & GRAINS

*P*erk up the flavor of brown rice and other longer-cooking grains with your choice
*of additions. Keep in mind that most seasonings work best when combined with
similarly flavored seasonings—sweet with sweet and savory with savory. Curry is
the exception—it unifies and complements both sweet and savory seasonings.*

Add one or more of the following items to taste *prior* to cooking:
- finely chopped kale or collard greens
- shredded or finely chopped carrots
- diced celery
- chopped onions
- sliced scallions
- raisins, currants, or other chopped dried fruit
- minced sun-dried tomatoes

Add one or more of the following seasonings to taste *after* cooking:
- peeled and finely chopped apple
- fresh lemon juice
- minced bell pepper
- chopped fresh parsley, basil, dill, cilantro, or mint
- natural soy sauce
- lemon, lime, or orange zest
- organic flax oil
- toasted nuts or seeds
- whole poppy seeds

Add a pinch or two to taste of one or more of the following spices or herbs *prior* to cooking:
- curry powder
- whole or ground fennel, caraway, or aniseed
- ground coriander
- cumin
- basil, dill, oregano, tarragon, or thyme
- crushed garlic
- Hungarian paprika
- fresh or ground ginger
- cinnamon
- whole cloves
- allspice
- crushed red chili peppers

Plain Basmati Rice

Yield: 3 to 4 servings

*B*asmati rice is an aromatic, long-grain, white rice with a fine texture. *Dubbed the "queen of fragrance," basmati has a perfumy aroma and nutlike flavor. It has been grown in the foothills of the Himalayas for thousands of years. You can find basmati rice in natural food stores, Indian and Middle Eastern markets, and some supermarkets. Brown basmati rice, also called Texmati, is a hybrid of long-grain brown rice and basmati rice.*

1 cup white basmati rice

1½ cups water for pressure cooker method;

2 cups water for standard stovetop method

1 Tablespoon canola oil or extra-virgin olive oil (optional)

½ teaspoon salt

Per serving: Calories 171, Protein 3 g, Fat 0 g, Carbohydrates 38 g

Pressure cooker method: Rinse and drain the rice well in a mesh strainer. Place the water, oil, if using, and salt in a 3½-quart or larger pressure cooker, and bring to a boil. Stir in the rice, lock the lid in place, and bring up to high pressure over high heat. Reduce the heat just enough to maintain high pressure, and cook for 3 minutes.

2. Remove from the heat and let the pressure come down naturally for 7 minutes to complete the cooking. Fluff and serve.

Standard stovetop method: Rinse and drain the rice well in a mesh strainer. Place the water, rice, oil, if using, and salt in a heavy saucepan. Bring to a boil. Immediately reduce the heat to very low, and cover. Cook undisturbed for 15 to 20 minutes. Do not peek inside the pot!

2. Remove from the heat, and stir up the grain so the drier kernels on top are mixed with the wetter ones on the bottom. Place a clean tea towel over the pot. Replace the lid snugly over the towel, and let rest for 5 to 10 minutes. The towel will absorb any excess moisture. Fluff again and serve.

BASIC QUINOA

Yield: 3 to 4 servings

*Q*uinoa is a tiny, quick-cooking grain with a mild flavor and fluffy texture. It has a higher protein content than corn, barley, or rice, and more calcium than cow's milk. It is rich in minerals and amino acids, such as lysine, and is easy to digest. Once the principal grain of the Incas, it has survived 400 years in remote, inaccessible areas of the Andes. Quinoa is sometimes called "vegetarian caviar" because of its soft, crunchy consistency and glistening grains. Quinoa is coated with a natural insect repellent called saponin, *which can be very bitter, so always rinse quinoa well in a fine mesh strainer before using.*

Pressure cooker method: Rinse and drain the quinoa well in a fine mesh strainer. Place the water and salt or soy sauce in a 3½-quart or larger pressure cooker, and bring to a boil. Stir in the quinoa, lock the lid in place, and start to bring up to high pressure over high heat. Begin timing for 2 minutes as soon as the lid is locked into place.

2. Remove from the heat after 2 minutes, whether or not high pressure has been reached. Let the pressure come down naturally for 10 minutes to complete the cooking. Fluff and serve.

Standard stovetop method: Rinse and drain the quinoa well in a fine mesh strainer. Place the water and salt or soy sauce in a medium saucepan, and bring to a boil. Stir in the quinoa, reduce heat to low, cover tightly, and simmer for 15 minutes or until tender. Do not stir the quinoa during cooking.

2. Remove from the heat, and stir up the grain so the drier kernels on top are mixed with the wetter ones on the bottom. Place a clean tea towel over the pot. Replace the lid snugly over the towel, and let rest for 5 minutes. The towel will absorb any excess moisture. Fluff and serve.

1 cup quinoa

1½ cups water for pressure cooker method;
   2 cups water for standard stovetop method

½ teaspoon salt, or natural soy sauce to taste

Per serving: Calories 173,
Protein 7 g, Fat 2 g,
Carbohydrates 30 g

95

BASIC BARLEY

Yield: 4 servings

*B*arley has a sweet, delicate flavor and a delightfully chewy texture. It is rich in minerals including iron, calcium, and potassium. Barley is also an excellent source of soluble fiber, which has been shown to be beneficial in reducing high cholesterol levels.

❦

1 cup pearled barley

2½ cups water for pressure cooker method; 3 cups water for standard stovetop method

1 Tablespoon canola oil (to help control foaming; optional for stovetop cooking)

½ teaspoon salt, or natural soy sauce to taste

Tips: For the most delicious, tender, and digestible barley, soak the barley in the recommended amount of water for 6 to 8 hours prior to cooking. Do not drain. To retain all the nutrients, always use the same water for cooking as for soaking.

Per serving: Calories 168, Protein 5 g, Fat 0 g, Carbohydrates 37 g

Pressure cooker method: Rinse and drain the barley well in a mesh strainer. Place the water, oil, and salt or soy sauce in a 3½-quart or larger pressure cooker, and bring to a boil. Stir in the barley, lock the lid in place, and bring up to high pressure over high heat. Reduce the heat just enough to maintain high pressure, and cook for 20 to 22 minutes.

2. Remove from the heat and let the pressure come down naturally for 10 to 15 minutes to complete the cooking. Fluff and serve.

Standard stovetop method: Rinse and drain the barley well in a mesh strainer. Place the water, oil, if using, and salt or soy sauce in a medium saucepan, and bring to boil. Stir in the barley, reduce the heat to low, cover tightly, and simmer for 30 to 40 minutes, or until tender. Do not stir during cooking.

2. Remove from the heat, and stir up the grain so the drier kernels on top are mixed with the wetter ones on the bottom. Place a clean tea towel over the pot. Replace the lid snugly over the towel, and let sit for 10 to 15 minutes. The towel will absorb any excess moisture. Fluff and serve.

BASIC BULGUR

Yield: 3 to 4 servings

Bulgur is made from whole wheat berries that have been hulled, cracked, steamed, dried, and crushed to create a texture similar to corn grits. Bulgur is available in several grinds. Medium grind is ideal because it's firm, hearty, and chewy.

Pressure cooker method: Place the water in a 3½-quart or larger pressure cooker, and bring to a boil. Stir in the bulgur and salt, lock the lid in place, and bring up to high pressure over high heat. Reduce the heat just enough to maintain high pressure, and cook for 5 minutes.

2. Remove from the heat and let the pressure come down naturally for 10 minutes to complete the cooking. Fluff and serve.

Standard stovetop method: Place the water and salt in a medium saucepan, and bring to a boil. Stir in the bulgur, reduce the heat to low, cover tightly, and simmer for 20 minutes. Do not stir the bulgur during cooking.

2. Remove from the heat, and stir up the grain so the drier kernels on top are mixed with the wetter ones on the bottom. Place a clean tea towel over the pot. Replace the lid snugly over the towel, and let rest for 5 minutes. The towel will absorb any excess moisture. Fluff and serve.

**1½ cups water for pressure cooker method;
2 cups water for standard stovetop method**

1 cup bulgur

½ teaspoon salt, or natural soy sauce to taste

Per serving: Calories 194,
Protein 7 g, Fat 0 g,
Carbohydrates 40 g

LEMON CURRY RICE

Yield: 4 servings

*T*his is one version of many different Mediterranean-style rice pilaf dishes that can be found throughout the Middle East and Greece. It makes a delicious side dish for virtually any vegetable or bean entrée.

1 cup brown rice

1 Tablespoon extra-virgin olive oil

2 cups water

1 to 1½ teaspoons curry powder

¼ teaspoon salt

2 to 3 Tablespoons fresh lemon juice

Pressure cooker method: Rinse and drain the rice well. Heat the oil in a 3½-quart or larger pressure cooker over medium heat. Add the rice and cook, stirring constantly, until the grains are coated with oil and begin to smell toasted, about 3 to 4 minutes.

2. Add the water, curry powder, and salt, and bring to a boil. Lock the lid in place, and bring up to high pressure over high heat. Reduce the heat just enough to maintain high pressure. Cook for 40 minutes. Remove from the heat and the pressure come down naturally for 10 minutes to complete the cooking. Stir in the fresh lemon juice, and serve.

Standard stovetop method: Rinse and drain the rice well. Heat the oil in a medium saucepan over medium heat. Add the rice and cook, stirring constantly, until the grains are coated with oil and begin to smell toasted, about 3 to 4 minutes.

2. Add the water, curry powder, and salt and bring to a boil. Reduce the heat to low, cover tightly, and simmer for 50 to 60 minutes. Do not stir during cooking.

3. Remove from the heat, add the lemon juice and salt, and stir up the grain so the drier kernels on top are mixed with the wetter ones on the bottom. Place a clean tea towel over the pot. Replace the lid snugly over the towel, and let rest for 10 minutes. The towel will absorb any excess moisture. Fluff and serve.

Per serving: Calories 90, Protein 1 g, Fat 4 g, Carbohydrates 13 g

Spanish Rice

Yield: 4 servings

*R*ice is nice with a touch of spice!

Pressure cooker method: Rinse and drain the rice well. Place the water, soy sauce, garlic, cumin, and salt in a 3½-quart or larger pressure cooker, and bring to a boil. Stir in the rice, lock the lid in place, and bring up to high pressure over high heat. Reduce the heat just enough to maintain high pressure. Cook for 40 minutes. Remove from the heat and let the pressure come down naturally for 10 minutes to complete the cooking.

2. Stir in the tomato, herbs, and olive oil. Fluff and serve.

Standard stovetop method: Rinse and drain the rice well. Place the water, soy sauce, garlic, cumin, and salt in a medium saucepan, and bring to boil. Stir in the rice, reduce heat to low, cover tightly, and simmer for 50 to 60 minutes. Do not stir the rice during cooking.

2. Remove from the heat. Stir up the grain so the drier kernels on top are mixed with the wetter ones on the bottom. Place a clean tea towel over the pot. Replace the lid snugly over the towel, and let rest for 10 minutes. The towel will absorb any excess moisture.

3. Stir in the tomato, herbs, and olive oil. Fluff and serve.

1 cup brown rice

2 cups water

1 Tablespoon natural soy sauce

1 teaspoon crushed garlic

1 teaspoon cumin

¼ teaspoon salt

1 fresh, ripe tomato, chopped

Chopped fresh cilantro or parsley, to taste

1 Tablespoon extra-virgin olive oil

Per serving: Calories 211, Protein 4 g, Fat 5 g, Carbohydrates 39 g

RED RIBBON RICE

Yield: 4 to 6 servings

*T*his rice dish is fragrant, festive, and easy to prepare, making it ideal for everyday meals or entertaining.

❧

1½ cups water for pressure cooker method;
1¾ cups water for standard stovetop method

½ cup raisins

1 Tablespoon nutritional yeast flakes

1 teaspoon fresh rosemary, or ¼ teaspoon dried rosemary

1 teaspoon crushed garlic

½ teaspoon salt

1 cup white basmati rice, rinsed and drained

1 small red bell pepper, sliced into matchsticks

½ cup coarsely chopped walnuts

1 Tablespoon organic flax oil or extra-virgin olive oil

Per serving: Calories 271,
Protein 5 g, Fat 9 g,
Carbohydrates 40 g

Pressure cooker method: Place the water, raisins, nutritional yeast, rosemary, garlic, and salt in a 3½-quart or larger pressure cooker, and bring to a boil. Stir in the rice. Lock the lid in place, and bring up to high pressure over high heat. Reduce the heat just enough to maintain high pressure, and cook for 3 minutes.

2. Remove from the heat and allow the pressure to come down naturally for 7 minutes to complete the cooking. Release any remaining pressure using a quick release method.

3. Stir in the bell pepper, walnuts, and oil, and fluff until evenly distributed.

Standard stovetop method: Place the water, raisins, nutritional yeast, rosemary, garlic, and salt in a 2-quart or larger saucepan, and bring to a boil. Stir in the rice, cover tightly, and simmer until almost all of the liquid has been absorbed, about 15 to 20 minutes.

2. Remove from the heat and stir up the rice so the drier kernels on top are mixed with the wetter ones on the bottom. Place a clean tea towel over the pot. Replace the lid snugly over the towel, and let rest for 5 minutes. The towel will absorb any excess moisture.

3. Stir in the bell pepper, walnuts, and oil, and fluff until evenly distributed.

100

Mushroom Barley Pilaf

Yield: 4 servings

*S*erve this hearty, soothing pilaf with a steamed green vegetable and a crisp salad for a very satisfying meal.

Pressure cooker method: Rinse and drain the barley well in a mesh strainer. Heat the oil in a 3½-quart or larger pressure cooker over medium heat. Add the onion and garlic, and sauté for 10 minutes. Stir in the barley, mushrooms, carrot, celery, soy sauce, and dill. Mix well.

2. Pour in the water and bring up to high pressure over high heat. Reduce the heat just enough to maintain high pressure. Cook for 20 to 22 minutes.

3. Remove from the heat and let the pressure come down naturally for 10 to 15 minutes to complete the cooking. Fluff and serve.

Standard stovetop method: Rinse and drain the barley well in a strainer. Heat the oil in a medium saucepan. Add the onion and garlic, and sauté for 10 minutes. Stir in the barley, mushrooms, carrot, celery, soy sauce, and dill, and mix well.

2. Pour in the water and bring to a boil. Reduce the heat to low, cover tightly, and simmer for 30 to 40 minutes or until tender. Do not stir the barley during cooking.

3. Remove from the heat, and stir up the grain so the drier kernels on top are mixed with the wetter ones on the bottom. Place a clean tea towel over the pot. Replace the lid snugly over the towel, and let rest for 10 to 15 minutes. The towel will absorb any excess moisture. Fluff and serve.

1 cup pearled barley

1 Tablespoon extra-virgin olive oil

1 large onion, chopped

½ teaspoon crushed garlic

2½ cups boiling water for pressure cooker method; 3 cups boiling water for standard stovetop method

1 cup coarsely chopped fresh mushrooms

1 large carrot, chopped

1 stalk celery, finely chopped

2 Tablespoons natural soy sauce

1 Tablespoon dill

Per serving: Calories 189, Protein 5 g, Fat 3 g, Carbohydrates 34 g

101

Basic Couscous

Yield: 3 to 4 servings

*C*ouscous is a quick-cooking, grain-like pasta that is great to have on hand for speedy salads and last-minute suppers. Use whole wheat couscous if you can find it, because it contains the wheat bran with the germ intact.

2 cups water

½ teaspoon salt

1 cup couscous

1. Place the water and salt in a medium saucepan, and bring to a boil. Reduce the heat to medium, stir in the couscous, and cook, stirring constantly, for 1 minute.

2. Remove from the heat, cover, and let sit for 5 minutes. Fluff with a fork before serving.

Per serving: Calories 156,
Protein 5 g, Fat 0 g,
Carbohydrates 34 g

MOROCCAN COUSCOUS

Yield: 4 to 6 servings

Quick-cooking couscous spiked with tantalizing spices makes an engaging side dish for any meal. For an exotic breakfast, omit the cumin, and serve with soymilk and extra sweetener, if desired.

1. Combine all the ingredients, except the couscous, in a 2-quart saucepan, and bring to a boil. Stir in the couscous, reduce the heat to low, cover, and simmer for 1 minute.

2. Remove from the heat and let sit covered for 5 to 10 minutes. Fluff with a fork and serve.

2 cups water

½ cup raisins

⅓ cup chopped walnuts

2 to 4 Tablespoons sugar

1 teaspoon cumin

½ teaspoon cinnamon

½ teaspoon ground ginger

½ teaspoon salt

¼ teaspoon turmeric

1 cup couscous

Per serving: Calories 227,
Protein 5 g, Fat 4 g,
Carbohydrates 42 g

Broccoli "Cheese" Grits

Yield: 2 to 4 servings

*A*lthough some might think it strange, hot polenta is great for breakfast. It also makes an interesting main meal or side dish. Nutritional yeast flakes add cheese-like undertones, while broccoli adds flavor, nutrition, and beautiful flecks of green.

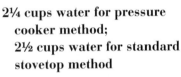

2¼ cups water for pressure cooker method;
2½ cups water for standard stovetop method

⅔ cup corn grits

½ to 1 cup finely chopped broccoli

2 Tablespoons nutritional yeast flakes

1 to 2 teaspoons extra-virgin olive oil

1 to 2 teaspoons organic flax oil

½ teaspoon salt

Pressure cooker method: Combine the water, grits, and broccoli in a 3½-quart or larger pressure cooker, and bring to a boil stirring constantly with a long-handled wooden spoon. Simmer, stirring constantly and briskly, until smooth and slightly thickened.

2. Lock the lid in place, and bring up to pressure over high heat. Adjust the heat to cook at low-pressure (8 lbs.) for 10 minutes. Remove from the heat and allow the pressure to come down naturally for 6 minutes to complete the cooking. Alternatively, cook at high pressure (15 lbs.) for 6 minutes and allow the pressure to come down naturally for 10 minutes.

3. Stir the polenta well, mixing in the broccoli and any liquid on top. Then stir in the nutritional yeast flakes, olive oil, flax oil, and salt, and mix until well combined.

Standard stovetop method: Bring the water to a boil in a heavy-bottomed saucepan. Add the broccoli and simmer for about 5 minutes or until tender. Remove from the heat and slowly stir in the grits, stirring briskly with a long-handled wooden

Per serving: Calories 196, Protein 5 g, Fat 5 g, Carbohydrates 33 g

spoon. Return to a boil, stirring constantly. Reduce the heat to very low, cover, and cook, stirring occasionally, for about 20 to 40 minutes, or until very thick.

2. Stir in the nutritional yeast flakes, olive oil, flax oil, and salt, and mix until well combined.

Tips: Do not be tempted to substitute cornmeal for the corn grits because you will not have good results. Use only the more coarsely ground, whole grain grits, sometimes called polenta, *which can be found in natural food stores and many supermarkets.*

If the polenta sticks to the bottom of your pressure cooker or saucepan, slip a flame tamer, also called a heat diffuser, underneath the pan while cooking. For less stirring and sticking using the stovetop method, after the grits and broccoli come to a boil, transfer the mixture to a double boiler to finish the cooking.

To round out your dinner, serve the grits with steamed carrots or sliced tomatoes topped with fresh basil. Add a tossed salad with baby greens, dressed with a splash of balsamic vinegar and extra-virgin olive oil.

⊕

CHAPTER VII

PIZZA, SANDWICHES & SPREADS

ROASTED VEGETABLE PIZZA
WITH TOMATO TINGED TOFU

Yield: 4 to 6 servings

*T*his is a long name for a very simple dish. Select a pizza crust, spread it with a well-seasoned tofu pâté, top it with your choice of seasonal vegetables, and bake it to golden perfection. Now who said healthful food is boring?

Tofu pâté:

½ pound firm regular tofu, rinsed, patted dry, and crumbled

2 Tablespoons tomato paste

2 Tablespoons extra-virgin olive oil

1 Tablespoon natural soy sauce

1 teaspoon ground fennel or dried basil

1 teaspoon oregano

1 teaspoon crushed garlic

⅛ to ¼ teaspoon cayenne pepper

Salt and pepper

Pizza crust options (choose one):

1 loaf French or Italian bread, 16 to 20 inches long, cut in half widthwise and lengthwise

1 French baguette, 18 to 22 inches long, cut in half widthwise and lengthwise

1 prebaked pizza shell, 15 inches in diameter, thawed to room temperature

Topping:

2 cups very finely sliced or chopped mixed vegetables

1 Tablespoon extra-virgin olive oil

1. Preheat the oven to 450°F. Place the crust on a dry baking sheet, pizza pan, or baking stone, and set aside.

2. Place all the pâté ingredients in a food processor, and blend into a smooth paste. Spread the mixture evenly over the crust.

3. Toss the vegetables with the olive oil until they are evenly coated. Distribute the vegetables evenly over the top of the pâté, and press them down lightly so they won't fall off.

4. Bake until the vegetables are golden brown, the tofu is hot, and the crust is crisp, about 10 to 15 minutes.

Tip: Some good vegetable choices include onions, zucchini, red or green bell pepper, roasted red peppers, mushrooms, water-packed artichoke hearts, scallions, shallots, firm ripe tomatoes, sliced olives, shredded carrots, and capers.

Per serving: Calories 488, Protein 15 g, Fat 15 g, Carbohydrates 60 g

CHICK-PEA & TOMATO PIZZA

Yield: 4 to 6 servings

*W*onderfully aromatic, a little bit spicy, and deliciously different from any pizza you've ever eaten.

1. Preheat the oven to 450°F. Place the crust on a dry baking sheet, pizza pan, or baking stone, and set aside.

2. Place all the pâté ingredients in a food processor, and blend into a smooth paste, using just enough water to facilitate processing. Spread the mixture evenly over the crust.

3. Cover the top generously and evenly with the tomato slices. Sprinkle the top of the tomatoes with the nutritional yeast flakes, if desired. Sprinkle the nutritional yeast directly on the tomatoes. Do not sprinkle it on the pâté because it will stick to the roof of your mouth when you eat it.

4. Bake until the crust is crisp, about 10 to 15 minutes.

Chick-pea pâté:

1½ cups cooked chick-peas, rinsed and drained

2 Tablespoons extra-virgin olive oil

2 Tablespoons water, as needed

1 Tablespoon balsamic vinegar

1 teaspoon crushed garlic

1 teaspoon oregano

½ teaspoon salt

¼ teaspoon pepper

⅛ teaspoon cayenne pepper

Pizza crust options (choose one):

1 loaf French or Italian bread, 16 to 20 inches long, cut in half widthwise and lengthwise

1 French baguette, 18 to 22 inches long, cut in half widthwise and lengthwise

1 prebaked pizza shell, 15 inches in diameter, thawed to room temperature

Topping:

3 to 4 large, ripe tomatoes, sliced

1 to 2 Tablespoons nutritional yeast flakes (optional)

Per serving: Calories 404,
Protein 15 g, Fat 10 g,
Carbohydrates 62 g

Asparagus & Mushroom Pizza

Yield: 4 to 6 servings

A ttractive and delicious, this recipe puts a gourmet but healthful spin on an American specialty.

❦

Tofu pizza cheeze:

½ pound firm regular tofu, rinsed, patted dry, and crumbled

4 Tablespoons sweet white miso

Pizza crust options (choose one):

1 loaf French or Italian bread, 16 to 20 inches long, cut in half widthwise and lengthwise

1 French baguette, 18 to 22 inches long, cut in half widthwise and lengthwise

15-inch prebaked pizza shell, thawed to room temperature

Vegetable topping:

3 to 4 Tablespoons grainy brown mustard

20 to 24 asparagus spears, cut diagonally into 1-inch pieces, and steamed until tender-crisp

1⅓ cups thinly sliced mushrooms

½ cup thinly sliced red onions

Salt and pepper

1 to 2 Tablespoons extra-virgin olive oil

1. Place the tofu in a medium mixing bowl. Add the miso and mash it into the tofu with a fork. Cover tightly and let rest in the refrigerator at least 30 minutes.

2. Preheat the oven to 450°F. Place the crust on a dry baking sheet, pizza pan, or baking stone.

3. Spread the mustard in a thin layer over the crust. Arrange the steamed asparagus, mushrooms, and onions in layers evenly over the mustard. Sprinkle each layer with a little salt and pepper. Lightly drizzle the vegetables with the oil. Scatter the pizza cheeze evenly over the vegetables, and press it down lightly so the topping won't fall off.

4. Bake until the topping is golden brown and the crust is crisp, about 10 to 15 minutes.

Per serving: Calories 457, Protein 16 g, Fat 9 g, Carbohydrates 73 g

*Variation: For **Mushroom & Onion Pizza**, omit the asparagus and use a few extra mushrooms and onion slices. Proceed as directed above.*

MONSTER MASH

Yield: about 1⅔ cups

This is a fun, creative spread that calls for a little ingenuity. Start with your choice of beans, and add one or more other ingredients to suit your taste. Make the spread as thick or thin as you like. Use the finished spread as a sandwich stuffer or tortilla filling, or as a dip for pita triangles and vegetables.

1. Place the beans in a food processor fitted with a metal blade, and process until they are ground.

2. Add the seasoning options of your choice, and process or pulse into a coarse paste, adding a little bean cooking liquid or water, as needed.

3. Adjust the seasonings to taste, and add more optional ingredients as necessary to achieve the flavor and texture you desire.

Beans:

1⅔ cups cooked beans, rinsed and drained (reserve cooking liquid)

Seasoning options:

Barbecue sauce	**Nutritional yeast flakes**
Bell pepper	**Olive oil (extra-virgin)**
Capers	**Onion**
Carrot	**Pepper**
Celery	**Pickles**
Chili sauce	**Pickle relish**
Citrus juice (lemon, lime, orange)	**Radishes**
Flax oil (organic)	**Salad dressing (nondairy)**
Garlic	**Salt**
Herbs	**Scallions**
Horseradish	**Seed butter**
Hot sauce	**Soy sauce (natural)**
Ketchup	**Spices**
Mayonnaise (vegan)	**Steak sauce**
Miso	**Tomato paste**
Mustard (prepared)	**Vegetables, cooked**
Nut butter	**Vinegar**

Per 2 tablespoons
(using pinto beans and no options):
Calories 30,
Protein 2 g, Fat 0 g,
Carbohydrates 6 g

111

MESSY MIKES

Yield: 4 servings

This quick sandwich staple is a tasty vegetarian version of Sloppy Joes.

❦

1 Tablespoon extra-virgin olive oil

1 medium onion, diced

8-ounce package tempeh, crumbled

2 Tablespoons natural soy sauce

½ cup ketchup

1 teaspoon prepared yellow mustard

1 teaspoon apple cider vinegar

1 teaspoon sugar

4 whole grain burger buns, split

1. Heat the oil in a medium saucepan over medium-high heat. Add the onion, tempeh, and soy sauce, and sauté until the onion is tender and golden brown, about 10 minutes.

2. Add the ketchup, mustard, vinegar, and sugar, and mix well. Reduce the heat to medium, and simmer uncovered 10 minutes, stirring often. Spoon the hot mixture between the buns and serve at once.

Per serving: Calories 312,
Protein 15 g, Fat 8 g,
Carbohydrates 44 g

SPINACH SALAD SANDWICHES

Yield: 2 sandwiches

*S*imple, simple, simple. Yet amazingly filling and delicious.

1. Stir together the cocktail sauce and mayonnaise. Spread over the bread slices.

2. Rinse the spinach well, and pat the leaves dry with a clean tea towel. Layer the spinach, mushrooms, and onion, if using, between the bread. Slice and serve.

2 Tablespoons cocktail sauce, barbecue sauce, or ketchup

2 Tablespoons Low-Fat, Egg-Free Mayonnaise, p. 128, or your favorite vegan mayonnaise

3 to 4 cups fresh spinach leaves, stems removed, lightly packed

½ to 1 cup sliced fresh mushrooms, raw or lightly sautéed (optional)

Thinly sliced red onion, raw or lightly sautéed (optional)

4 thick slices of whole grain bread

Per serving: Calories 178,
Protein 6 g, Fat 5 g,
Carbohydrates 25 g

Bean Burritos

Yield: 4 burritos

*B*ean *burritos are always fun to construct. They make a satisfying quick lunch or dinner. Some independent thinkers even like them for breakfast!*

❦

Bean filling:

1½ cups cooked pinto beans, rinsed and drained

½ cup tomato sauce

1 teaspoon chili powder

¼ teaspoon garlic powder

¼ teaspoon cumin

¼ teaspoon oregano

Several drops bottled hot sauce

4 whole wheat flour tortillas (lard-free)

Topping options:

Shredded carrot

Fresh cilantro

Shredded lettuce

Chopped onions

Sliced black olives

Sliced scallions

Tofu Sour Cream, p. 129

Chopped tomato

Per serving: Calories 177,
Protein 7 g, Fat 2 g,
Carbohydrates 32 g

1. Combine the filling ingredients in a medium saucepan, and bring to a boil. Reduce the heat to medium, and simmer uncovered for 5 minutes, stirring occasionally. Remove from the heat. Mash the beans coarsely with the back of a wooden spoon, a fork, or a potato masher. Cover and set aside.

2. Warm the tortillas by placing one at a time in a dry skillet over medium heat, just until the tortilla is warm to the touch, about 1 minute. Immediately remove it from the skillet, lay it on a flat surface, and cover with a clean tea towel to keep it warm. Warm the remaining tortillas in the same fashion.

3. Spoon ¼ of the bean mixture onto each of the tortillas, placing it in a strip along one side, slightly off center. Add your favorite toppings, and roll the tortilla around the filling.

Garbanzo Sandwich Salad

Yield: 4 servings

For an attractive luncheon, scoop this salad onto lettuce-lined plates, garnish it with a little paprika, and surround it with fresh tomato wedges. Alternatively, spread it on whole grain bread, or stuff it into whole wheat pita pockets, along with lettuce and fresh tomato slices.

Place the beans in a medium bowl, and mash well. Add the remaining ingredients and stir until well combined. Chill thoroughly before serving.

1⅔ cups cooked garbanzo beans, rinsed and drained

½ cup diced celery or grated carrot

2 to 3 Tablespoons Low-Fat Egg-Free Mayonnaise, p. 128, or your favorite vegan mayonnaise

1 scallion, thinly sliced

2 Tablespoons minced fresh parsley (optional)

2 teaspoons well-drained pickle relish

2 teaspoons grainy brown mustard

Salt

Per serving: Calories 143, Protein 5 g, Fat 4 g, Carbohydrates 21 g

KALE & KRAUT SANDWICHES

Yield: 4 servings

*H*umble kale and tangy sauerkraut reach exciting culinary heights when married in this simple but tempting sandwich.

❦

12 to 16 large, whole kale leaves, cleaned and stems removed

8 slices whole grain bread, toasted if desired

3 to 4 Tablespoons tahini

3 to 4 Tablespoons Dijon mustard

1 cup low-sodium sauerkraut, very well drained

1. Fill a large pot or Dutch oven with water, and bring to a boil. Parboil the whole kale leaves, several at a time, for 3 to 4 minutes. Remove with a slotted spoon, and parboil the next batch. Continue in this fashion until all the kale is parboiled. Drain well and pat dry.

2. Spread half the bread with the tahini and the other half with the mustard. Layer the cooked kale and sauerkraut between the bread. Slice and serve.

Per serving: Calories 224,
Protein 7 g, Fat 10 g,
Carbohydrates 25 g

NORTH COUNTRY BEAN PÂTÉ

Yield: about 2 cups

*A*n *incredibly quick and easy-to-make low-fat spread that doubles as a party dip.*

Place all the ingredients in a food processor fitted with a metal blade, and process until smooth. Chill thoroughly before serving.

1¾ cups cooked great Northern beans, rinsed and drained

½ to 1 cup whole grain bread crumbs

¼ cup sliced scallions

2 Tablespoons fresh lemon juice

1 Tablespoon organic flax oil or extra-virgin olive oil

1 Tablespoon natural soy sauce

1½ teaspoons Dijon mustard

½ teaspoon crushed garlic

½ teaspoon basil

½ teaspoon dill

Tips: *Either fresh or dry bread crumbs may be used. If a stiffer spread is preferred, gradually add more bread crumbs while processing until the desired consistency is achieved.*

Per ¼ cup serving: Calories 77, Protein 3 g, Fat 2 g, Carbohydrates 10 g

Hummus

Yield: about 2 cups

*T**he best of the beloved bean dips!*

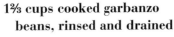

1⅔ cups cooked garbanzo
   beans, rinsed and drained

¼ cup tahini

3 Tablespoons fresh lemon
   juice

1 Tablespoon organic flax oil
   or extra-virgin olive oil

Water or bean cooking liquid,
   as needed

½ teaspoon crushed garlic

¼ teaspoon cumin

¼ teaspoon coriander

¼ teaspoon paprika

⅛ teaspoon salt

Pinch of cayenne pepper

2 sprigs fresh parsley, stems
   removed

1. Place the beans in a food processor fitted with a metal blade, and process until they are ground.

2. Add the tahini, lemon juice, and oil, and process into a coarse paste, adding about a tablespoon of water, only if necessary, to facilitate processing. The mixture should be very thick.

3. Add the remaining ingredients, except the parsley, and blend thoroughly. Pulse in the parsley until it is chopped and evenly distributed.

Per ¼ cup serving: Calories 115,
Protein 4 g, Fat 6 g,
Carbohydrates 12 g

118

Peanut Whip

Yield: 2 to 3 servings

Yes, it's still possible to have your peanut butter and eat it too, even if you're watching your fat intake. The secrets are moderation and learning how to stretch fats so they are not so concentrated. In this recipe, high-fat peanut butter is extended with natural applesauce, adding just a touch of sweetness without diminishing the rich peanut flavor. It's a great sandwich or bagel spread, and is terrific on rice cakes topped with raisins. For a quick snack or company hors d'oeuvres, stuff it into crisp celery stalks.

Combine the applesauce and peanut butter in a small bowl, and stir together until well combined. Store any leftovers in the refrigerator.

3 to 4 Tablespoons unsweetened applesauce

2 Tablespoons natural peanut butter

Tips: This recipe is easily doubled. You'll have the best results if the peanut butter is at room temperature, and both the peanut butter and applesauce are thick rather than runny. If either is thin, use the smaller amount of applesauce.

Per serving: Calories 85,
Protein 4 g, Fat 6 g,
Carbohydrates 5 g

119

HAPPY HEN SALAD

Yield: about 2½ cups

*K*eep your heart healthy and the hens happy by using this tofu-based spread *instead of egg salad. It's a cinch to prepare and makes a terrific sandwich filling.*

❦

1 pound regular tofu, rinsed

½ cup diced celery

½ to 1 cup Low-Fat Egg-Free Mayonnaise, p. 128, or your favorite vegan mayonnaise

2 Tablespoons minced fresh parsley (optional)

2 teaspoons well-drained pickle relish

⅛ teaspoon turmeric

Grated onion or onion powder

Salt and pepper

1. Place the tofu in a saucepan with enough water to cover, and bring to a boil. Reduce the heat, cover, and simmer for 10 minutes. Drain and place in a bowl of ice water to cool. Drain well and press gently to remove any excess water. Pat dry. Transfer to a bowl, and mash using your hands.

2. Add the celery, mayonnaise, parsley, if using, pickle relish, and turmeric. Season with grated onion or onion powder, and salt and pepper to taste. Stir until well combined. Chill thoroughly before serving.

Per ¼ cup serving: Calories 82,
Protein 3 g, Fat 5 g,
Carbohydrates 2 g

120

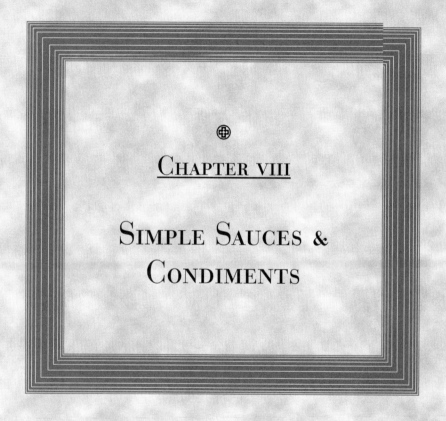

CHAPTER VIII

SIMPLE SAUCES & CONDIMENTS

Tomato Pasta Sauce

Yield: about 1 quart

*T*his simple but amazing pasta sauce doesn't take long to simmer, yet it has a rich, cooked-all-day flavor.

❧

2 Tablespoons extra-virgin olive oil

1 cup finely chopped onions

1 Tablespoon crushed garlic

28-ounce can chopped tomatoes (4 cups), undrained

6-ounce can tomato paste (⅔ cup)

1 teaspoon basil

½ teaspoon salt

¼ teaspoon oregano

¼ teaspoon rosemary

¼ teaspoon pepper

1. Heat the oil in a medium saucepan over medium-high. Add the onions and garlic, and sauté until golden brown and tender, about 10 minutes.

2. Add the tomatoes, including the juice, along with the remaining ingredients. Simmer, stirring occasionally, for 20 minutes. Serve hot over your favorite pasta.

Tips: *If time permits, allow the sauce to rest, covered, at room temperature for about an hour after cooking. This will allow the flavors to further develop and blend. Reheat before serving.*

If desired, 4 cups diced, fresh tomatoes may be substituted for the canned tomatoes. Fresh herbs may also be substituted for the dried herbs. Use 1 tablespoon chopped fresh basil, 1 teaspoon chopped fresh oregano, and 1 teaspoon chopped fresh rosemary.

Per ½ cup serving: Calories 71, Protein 2 g, Fat 2 g, Carbohydrates 8 g

VELVETY CHEEZE SAUCE

Yield: about 2½ cups

*U*se this velvety, ultra-low-fat, cheddar-style sauce on vegetables, pasta, rice, or toast. You'll be amazed how deceptively rich tasting and delicious it is despite its simplicity.

1. Place the potato, water, carrots, onions, and garlic in a medium saucepan, and bring to a boil. Reduce the heat to medium, cover, and simmer, stirring once or twice, until the vegetables are tender, about 10 minutes.

2. Transfer the cooked vegetables, their cooking liquid, and the remaining ingredients to a blender, and purée in batches into a completely smooth sauce.

3. Rinse out the saucepan and return the blended mixture to it. Warm the sauce over low, stirring often until hot.

1 medium potato, peeled and coarsely chopped

¾ cup water

½ cup chopped carrots

½ cup chopped onions

½ to 1 teaspoon crushed garlic

¾ cup silken tofu, crumbled

⅓ cup nutritional yeast flakes

1 Tablespoon fresh lemon juice

1 teaspoon salt

Per ½ cup serving: Calories 79, Protein 7 g, Fat 1 g, Carbohydrates 12 g

123

GOLDEN GRAVY

Yield: about 1½ cups

*N*utritional yeast flakes impart a captivating flavor filled with homey warmth. Use this lovely sauce on vegetables, potatoes, or grains. No one will suspect it's actually good for them!

¼ cup whole grain flour (whole wheat, barley, rye, or spelt)

¼ cup nutritional yeast flakes

¼ teaspoon onion powder

⅛ teaspoon pepper

1½ cups hot vegetable stock or water

2 Tablespoons natural soy sauce

1 Tablespoon extra-virgin olive oil

1. Toast the flour and nutritional yeast flakes in a dry medium saucepan over medium heat, stirring constantly until golden brown and fragrant.

2. Remove the saucepan from the heat, and stir in the onion powder and pepper. Gradually whisk in the hot stock or water, soy sauce, and oil, and beat until the gravy is very smooth.

3. Cook over medium heat, stirring almost constantly with the wire whisk, until thickened, smooth, and bubbly.

Per ¼ cup serving: Calories 57, Protein 3 g, Fat 2 g, Carbohydrates 6 g

HERBED BROWN GRAVY

Yield: about 1½ cups

A luscious, creamy, all-purpose gravy that's as tempting on tofu, tempeh, and veggie burgers as it is on potatoes, rice, and grains.

1. Combine the starch and soy sauce in a medium saucepan. Mix well to make a smooth, thin paste. Gradually whisk in the stock or water and dried herbs. Cook over medium-high heat, stirring constantly with a wire whisk, until thickened and bubbly.

2. Remove from the heat and vigorously whisk in the tahini. Best served at once.

2 Tablespoons cornstarch, arrowroot, or kuzu

3 Tablespoons natural soy sauce

1⅓ cups vegetable stock or water

Tiny pinch *each*: dried sage, thyme, rosemary, and oregano

2 Tablespoons tahini

Per ¼ cup serving: Calories 44,
Protein 2 g, Fat 2 g,
Carbohydrates 4 g

ROASTED RED PEPPER SAUCE

Yield: about 1½ cups

This no-cook sauce can be ready in mere minutes. With its simple ingredients, ease of preparation, and phenomenal taste, it will be love at first bite. Spoon it over pasta, grains, rice, or potatoes. It's also superb on vegetables, tofu, tempeh, beans, and even salads. In other words, dog-ear this page and make this sauce a staple recipe, because you can use it on practically everything!

❦

1 cup roasted red bell peppers, drained

½ cup silken tofu, crumbled

2 Tablespoons fresh lemon juice

1 Tablespoon extra-virgin olive oil

1 Tablespoon organic flax oil

1 Tablespoon sweet white miso

¼ teaspoon crushed garlic

¼ teaspoon *each*: pepper, dry mustard, and ground ginger

Pinch of salt

Combine all the ingredients in a blender, and process until smooth.

Per ¼ cup serving: Calories 60, Protein 1 g, Fat 5 g, Carbohydrates 3 g

Tip: *Roasted red bell peppers are available in cans or jars at supermarkets and Italian grocery stores.*

No-Cook Barbecue Sauce

Yield: about 1¼ cups

A quick, scrumptious barbecue sauce for beans, tempeh and tofu—with no cooking required!

Combine all the ingredients in a small bowl, and whisk them together until well blended.

⅓ cup tomato paste

¼ cup natural soy sauce

¼ cup apple cider vinegar

¼ cup pure maple syrup

2 teaspoons extra-virgin olive oil

2 teaspoons organic flax oil

1 teaspoon dry mustard

1 teaspoon crushed garlic

¼ teaspoon pepper

Several drops bottled hot sauce

Per ¼ cup serving: Calories 98,
Protein 2 g, Fat 3 g,
Carbohydrates 15 g

Low-Fat Egg-Free Mayonnaise I

Yield: about 1½ cups

*M*ayonnaise has a well-deserved reputation for being delicious but ultra-high in fat and cholesterol. Try these tasty, egg-free versions, and indulge to your heart's content.

1½ cups silken tofu, crumbled

3 Tablespoons fresh lemon juice

½ teaspoon salt

¼ teaspoon dry mustard

2 Tablespoons canola oil

1 Tablespoon organic flax oil

1. Place the tofu, lemon juice, salt, and mustard in a blender, and process until smooth and creamy.

2. With the blender running, drizzle in the oil in a slow, steady stream through the cap opening in the blender lid. Store in the refrigerator. It will keep for at least a week.

Per tablespoon: Calories 23,
Protein 1 g, Fat 2 g,
Carbohydrates 0 g

Low-Fat Egg-Free Mayonnaise II

Yield: about 1½ cups

1½ cups silken tofu, crumbled

2 teaspoons fresh lemon juice

2 teaspoons apple cider vinegar

1 teaspoon sugar

½ teaspoon prepared yellow mustard

½ teaspoon salt

1 Tablespoon extra-virgin olive oil

1 Tablespoon organic flax oil

1. Place the tofu, lemon juice, vinegar, sugar, mustard, and salt in a blender, and process until smooth and creamy.

2. With the blender running, drizzle in the oil in a slow, steady stream through the cap opening in the blender lid. Store in the refrigerator. It will keep for at least a week.

Per tablespoon: Calories 18,
Protein 1 g, Fat 2 g,
Carbohydrates 0 g

Horseradish Cocktail Sauce

Yield: about ⅓ cup

*D*evilishly good and deliciously fat-free!

Combine all the ingredients in a small bowl, and stir until well combined. Chill thoroughly before serving.

⅓ cup tomato paste

1½ Tablespoons prepared yellow mustard

1 Tablespoon prepared white horseradish (not creamed)

2 teaspoons fresh lemon juice

2 teaspoons apple cider vinegar

2 teaspoons natural soy sauce

2 teaspoons water

2 teaspoons sugar

Several drops bottled hot sauce

Per tablespoon: Calories 31, Protein 1 g, Fat 1 g, Carbohydrates 6 g

Tofu Sour Cream

Yield: about 1½ cups

*U*se this luscious dairy-free topping wherever you would typically use dairy sour cream. It has a magnificent taste and is so simple to prepare.

1. Place the tofu, lemon juice, vinegar, salt, and coriander in a blender, and process until smooth and creamy.

2. With the blender running, drizzle in the oil in a slow, steady stream through the cap opening in the blender lid. Store in the refrigerator. It will keep for at least a week.

1½ cups silken tofu, crumbled

2 Tablespoons fresh lemon juice

1 Tablespoon white wine vinegar

½ teaspoon salt

⅛ teaspoon ground coriander

2 Tablespoons canola oil

Per 2 tablespoons: Calories 72, Protein 3 g, Fat 6 g, Carbohydrates 2 g

129

FLAX SPRINKLES

*T*his tasty topping is a convenient way to get the healthful benefits of flaxseeds
and omega-3 fatty acids into your diet.

❧

Chili Sprinkles:

1 teaspoon ground flaxseeds

**1 teaspoon nutritional yeast
flakes**

¼ teaspoon chili powder

Curry Sprinkles:

1 teaspoon ground flaxseeds

**1 teaspoon nutritional yeast
flakes**

¼ teaspoon curry powder

> Per teaspoon (Chili & Curry):
> Calories 48,
> Protein 1 g, Fat 4 g,
> Carbohydrates 1 g

Sweet Sprinkles:
*(good for topping cold or hot
breakfast cereals, french toast,
and pancakes):*

1 teaspoon ground flaxseeds

1 teaspoon sugar

⅛ to ¼ teaspoon cinnamon

**Tiny pinch of nutmeg
(optional)**

> Per teaspoon (Sweet): Calories 55,
> Protein 0 g, Fat 4 g,
> Carbohydrates 4 g

You can grind the flaxseeds in a dry blender or electric coffee or grain mill. Although ground flaxseeds are easier to digest than the whole seeds, grinding exposes the volatile oils that are sensitive to air and light. Therefore, grind the seeds in small batches and store them in an airtight container in the freezer to prevent nutritional deterioration and rancidity. You do not need to defrost the ground seeds. Simply measure out the amount you need, and return the remainder to the freezer. Mix up the sprinkles right before you're ready to use them, and prepare just the amount you plan to use at that meal. Quantities can be increased with ease.

130

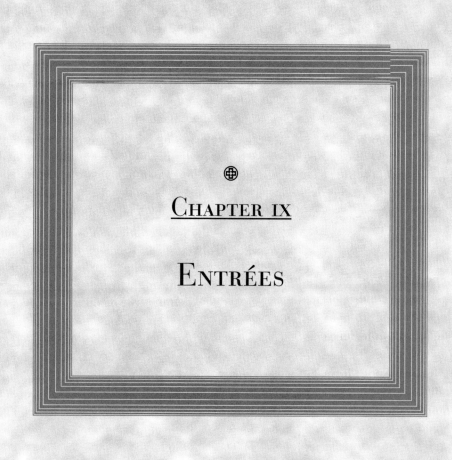

⊕

Chapter ix

Entrées

SPANISH-STYLE TOFU ESCABÈCHE

Yield: 4 servings

In Mediterranean countries, escabèche is made with poached or fried fish, which is preserved in a spicy marinade, refrigerated for at least twenty-four hours, and served cold. Each country has its own unique version of the dish, incorporating special flavors of the region. Firm tofu makes a delicious replacement for the fish. Fresh tomato slices topped with slivers of fresh basil would make a lovely accompaniment.

1 pound firm regular tofu, rinsed and patted dry

1 teaspoon crushed garlic

¾ teaspoon salt

½ teaspoon ground ginger

½ teaspoon pepper

Pinch of saffron (optional)

¼ cup wine vinegar

¼ cup finely minced shallots or onions

3 Tablespoons fresh lemon juice

1½ Tablespoons extra-virgin olive oil

1 large lemon, sliced

1. Steam the tofu for 10 minutes. Cool, then cut into ¾ x 3½-inch sticks. Place in a single layer in a wide, shallow glass or ceramic baking dish.

2. Place the garlic in a small bowl. Stir in the salt, ginger, pepper, and saffron, if using. Add the vinegar, shallots or onions, lemon juice, and olive oil, and mix well. Pour over the tofu. Layer the lemon slices over the tofu. Cover tightly and refrigerate a minimum of 8 hours or overnight. Serve cold with the lemon slices or extra lemon, if desired.

Per serving: Calories 143,
Protein 8 g, Fat 9 g,
Carbohydrates 5 g

132

Tofu Scrambola

Yield: 4 servings

*Y*ou'll never miss eggs again once you taste this hearty, cholesterol-free dish. Turmeric imparts a beautiful golden color, and nutritional yeast flakes add a delicious egg-like flavor. Tofu Scrambola is wonderful for leisurely breakfasts, brunches, lunches, and dinners.

1. Heat the oil in a large skillet over medium-high heat. When the oil is hot, add the carrots, peppers, scallions, and turmeric, and sauté for 3 to 4 minutes.

2. Add the tofu, nutritional yeast flakes, salt, and pepper. Mix well and continue to cook over medium heat, stirring constantly, for 5 to 7 minutes or until hot. Stir in the parsley, if using, and mix well. Serve at once.

1 Tablespoon extra-virgin olive oil

½ cup grated carrots

½ cup diced bell peppers

½ cup finely sliced scallions

¼ teaspoon turmeric

1 pound firm regular tofu, rinsed, patted dry and crumbled

2 Tablespoons nutritional yeast flakes

Seasoned salt (such as Spike) and pepper

2 Tablespoons minced fresh parsley (optional)

Per serving: Calories 138, Protein 10 g, Fat 8 g, Carbohydrates 6 g

FILET OF POACHED TOFU WITH TUNISIAN SPICES

Yield: 4 servings

This is a simple, quick dish with a delightful array of flavors.

❧

2 Tablespoons extra-virgin olive oil

2 teaspoons crushed garlic

2 teaspoons caraway

1 teaspoon coriander

1 teaspoon paprika

Salt, pepper, and cayenne pepper

Pinch of saffron threads (optional)

1 cup water

1 pound extra-firm regular tofu, rinsed, patted dry, and cut into 16 equal pieces

Fresh lemon juice

Lemon wedges

1. Heat the oil in a large skillet or Dutch oven. Sauté the garlic for 30 seconds over medium-low heat. Stir in the caraway, coriander, paprika, salt, pepper, cayenne, and saffron, if using. Pour in the water, mix well, and bring to a boil. Add the tofu, reduce the heat, cover, and simmer gently for 15 to 20 minutes, basting occasionally.

2. Remove the tofu with a slotted spoon, and place it on a serving platter. Strain the cooking liquid and add lemon juice to taste. Pass this sauce along with lemon wedges for individual seasoning at the table.

Per serving: Calories 146, Protein 8 g, Fat 11 g, Carbohydrates 2 g

Italian-Style Tofu Steaks with Fennel

Yield: 4 servings

*F*ennel becomes sweet and fragrant as it cooks, making it a tasty accompaniment to tofu.

1. Heat the oil in a large skillet. Add the garlic and sauté over medium heat for 1 minute. Add the fennel, salt, and pepper. Cover and cook over low heat, stirring occasionally, until just tender-crisp.

2. Lightly salt and pepper the tofu steaks on both sides. Place the tofu on top of the fennel. Cover and cook over medium heat for 5 to 7 minutes. Turn the steaks over and cook 5 to 7 minutes longer. Sprinkle with the fennel tops or parsley, and serve with lemon wedges on the side.

2 Tablespoons extra-virgin olive oil

1 teaspoon crushed garlic

4 medium fennel bulbs, trimmed and thinly sliced

Salt or seasoned salt (such as Spike) and pepper

1 pound firm regular tofu, rinsed, patted dry, and sliced into ½-inch-thick steaks

2 Tablespoons chopped fennel tops or minced fresh parsley

Lemon wedges

Per serving: Calories 163, Protein 9 g, Fat 12 g, Carbohydrates 4 g

135

SPICY TOFU STEAKS
WITH FRESH TOMATO SAUCE

Yield: 4 servings

*T*ofu is marinated in a piquant dressing then topped with a light and spicy tomato sauce.

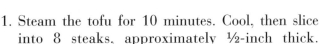

Tofu steaks:

1 pound firm regular tofu, rinsed and patted dry

Marinade:

½ cup fresh lemon juice

½ cup chopped onions

½ teaspoon salt

½ teaspoon cumin

½ teaspoon paprika

¼ teaspoon pepper

⅛ to ¼ teaspoon cayenne pepper

1. Steam the tofu for 10 minutes. Cool, then slice into 8 steaks, approximately ½-inch thick. Arrange in a single layer in a large, non-metallic baking dish.

2. Combine the marinade ingredients in a food processor or blender. Pour over the tofu, cover, and marinate in the refrigerator for at least 1 hour, or preferably 8 hours or overnight.

3. Preheat the oven to 350°F. Remove the tofu from the marinade, and place it in a single layer on an oiled baking sheet. Bake for 30 minutes.

4. Meanwhile, combine the sauce ingredients in a large saucepan. Bring to a boil, reduce the heat slightly, and simmer until thick, about 30 minutes. Adjust the seasonings, if necessary. Serve the hot tofu steaks topped with the tomato sauce.

Per serving: Calories 165,
Protein 10 g, Fat 9 g,
Carbohydrates 11 g

Tips: *To peel a tomato, first use a sharp knife to cut a small cross on the bottom of the tomato. Turn the tomato over, and cut out the core. Immerse the tomato in a pot of boiling water until the skin starts to curl, about 20 seconds. Remove the tomato from the pot using a slotted spoon, and transfer it to a bowl of cold water. Let it rest for 2 minutes until it can be handled comfortably. Remove the tomato from the cold water, and peel off the skin using your fingers. It should peel away easily.*

To seed a tomato, cut the tomato into quarters and gently scoop out the seeds with a spoon.

Fresh tomato sauce:

4 ripe tomatoes, peeled, seeded, and chopped

½ cup minced fresh parsley

1 Tablespoon extra-virgin olive oil

1 teaspoon paprika

½ teaspoon crushed garlic

½ teaspoon cumin

⅛ to ¼ teaspoon cayenne pepper

Salt and pepper

TOFU BROCHETTES

Yield: 4 to 6 servings

*G*rilled or broiled tofu kabobs are as much fun to make as they are to eat. The skewered tofu is alternated with chunks of colorful vegetables. Serve the brochettes and vegetables on a bed of cooked barley, rice, or millet.

Tofu brochettes:

1 pound extra-firm regular tofu, rinsed and patted dry

½ cup silken tofu, crumbled

½ cup fresh lime juice

2 Tablespoons fresh lemon juice

2 Tablespoons extra-virgin olive oil

1 teaspoon *each*: salt, turmeric, and crushed garlic

½ teaspoon *each*: cardamom and cumin

¼ teaspoon *each*: allspice and pepper

Vegetable options:

Mushrooms, whole if small or halved if large

Tomato chunks or whole cherry tomatoes

Onion chunks or peeled, whole pearl onions

Bell pepper, cut into large pieces

Zucchini chunks

1. Simmer the tofu in water, or steam it for 10 minutes; cool. Cut the tofu into large cubes, about 1½ inches, and place in a non-metallic baking dish large enough to hold the tofu in a single layer.

2. Combine the remaining ingredients, except the vegetable options, in a blender or food processor, and blend until creamy and smooth. Pour over the tofu, and turn each piece so it is coated all over. Cover and marinate in the refrigerator 4 to 24 hours, turning the pieces occasionally and spooning the marinade over them.

3. Skewer the tofu, alternating with the vegetables of your choice. Grill over an open flame or broil on a tray in the oven, occasionally turning and basting with the marinade, if desired, until golden, about 8 to 15 minutes.

Per serving (using tofu only): Calories 140,
Protein 8 g, Fat 9 g,
Carbohydrates 4 g

Turkish-Style Tempeh with Cumin

Yield: 3 to 4 servings

*S*erve this pungent dish with basmati rice and a tossed green salad on the side.

❧

1. Heat the oil in a large skillet. Add the onion, celery, garlic, and salt. Sauté over medium heat until the onion begins to color, about 15 minutes.

2. Add the lemon zest, cumin, pepper, and cayenne. Stir to distribute evenly, then stir in the tempeh cubes. Pour in the water and bring to a rapid boil over high heat. Cover, reduce the heat to medium, and simmer for 20 minutes, stirring once or twice.

3. Stir in the cilantro or parsley just before serving. Serve hot or cool with lemon wedges on the side.

1 Tablespoon extra-virgin olive oil

1 medium onion, chopped

¼ cup finely chopped celery

1 teaspoon crushed garlic

½ teaspoon salt

1 Tablespoon lemon zest

1 teaspoon ground cumin

Pinch of pepper

Pinch of cayenne pepper

8-ounce package tempeh, cut into ½-inch cubes

1 cup water

¼ cup chopped fresh cilantro or parsley

Lemon wedges

Tip: *Zest is the colored portion of the peel of citrus fruits which does not include the bitter white portion beneath it. You can remove it with a sharp paring knife or with a special citrus zester, available in supermarkets, cookware shops, and department stores.*

Per serving: Calories 185, Protein 11 g, Fat 8 g, Carbohydrates 16 g

Baked Tempeh with Tomatoes, Garlic & Sweet Pepper

Yield: 3 to 4 servings

*T*his dish is vibrant both in color and flavor. Leftovers are delicious served cold the following day.

❦

1 Tablespoon extra-virgin olive oil

2 teaspoons crushed garlic

1 large red bell pepper, cut into 1-inch pieces

2 large, ripe tomatoes, peeled, seeded, and coarsely chopped (see Tips p. 137)

½ teaspoon basil

Salt and pepper

8-ounce package tempeh

1. Heat the oil in a large skillet. Sauté the garlic for 1 minute over medium-low heat. Stir in the bell pepper, and sauté for 5 minutes. Add the tomatoes, basil, salt, and pepper. Continue to sauté 3 to 5 minutes longer. Preheat the oven to 400°F.

2. Lightly oil a medium casserole dish, and lay the whole piece of tempeh in the middle. Spread the tomato and pepper mixture over the tempeh. Cover tightly and bake for 20 to 30 minutes.

3. Remove from the oven and transfer the tempeh to a warm serving platter, leaving behind the tomato and pepper sauce. Transfer the sauce to a medium saucepan, and reduce it over high heat for a few minutes. Spoon the sauce around the tempeh. To serve, spoon a generous helping of sauce over each portion of tempeh.

Per serving: Calories 182, Protein 11 g, Fat 8 g, Carbohydrates 15 g

Sweet & Sour Tempeh

Yield: 4 servings

A notable entrée that always receives rave reviews. Serve it with a cooked grain of your choice. Basmati rice is particularly delicious with this dish, although brown rice, barley, or quinoa work well too.

1. Heat the oil in a large skillet. Add the tempeh and cook for 15 to 20 minutes, stirring almost constantly, until browned all over.

2. Add the carrots, peppers, and garlic, and sauté them with the tempeh until the peppers are tender.

3. Drain the pineapple but reserve ½ cup of the juice. Place the reserved juice and the remaining ingredients, except the pineapple chunks and scallions, in a small bowl or measuring cup. Mix until well combined. Pour over the tempeh and vegetables, then add the pineapple chunks. Cook, stirring constantly, until the sauce is just thickened, about 2 minutes. Serve hot, garnished with the scallions, if desired.

2 Tablespoons extra-virgin olive oil

8-ounce package tempeh, cut into cubes

1 cup grated carrots

1 red bell pepper, sliced into strips

1 green bell pepper, sliced into strips

½ teaspoon crushed garlic

2 cups canned pineapple chunks, packed in juice

¼ cup apple cider vinegar

¼ cup water

1 Tablespoon sugar

2 Tablespoons natural soy sauce

1 Tablespoon cornstarch

1 teaspoon ground ginger

2 scallions, thinly sliced (optional)

Per serving: Calories 296, Protein 11 g, Fat 10 g, Carbohydrates 38 g

141

Beans & Greens

Yield: 4 servings

*T*his simple combination creates a beautiful dish with a heavenly blend of flavors. Serve the mixture as a main dish with rice or another grain on the side. It also makes an excellent topping for warm corn bread or a delicious filling for pita pockets, tortillas, or chapatis.

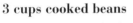

3 cups cooked beans

½ teaspoon crushed garlic

4 cups chopped kale, stems and center ribs removed, lightly packed

1 to 2 Tablespoons extra-virgin olive oil

Salt and pepper, to taste

1. Drain the beans but reserve 1 cup of the cooking liquid (see Tips below). Place the beans and the reserved cooking liquid in a large saucepan or Dutch oven. Stir in the garlic. Place the chopped kale on top of the beans, and bring to a boil. Cover, reduce the heat to low, and simmer for 15 to 18 minutes, or until the kale is tender.

2. Remove from the heat and stir in the oil, salt, and pepper to taste.

Per serving: Calories 247, Protein 11 g, Fat 6 g, Carbohydrates 37 g

Tips: *If the beans are not organic or are heavily salted, drain and rinse them, then drain them again. Substitute 1 cup vegetable stock or water for the bean cooking liquid.*

Spinach & Garbanzo Curry

Yield: 4 servings

Rich and spicy, this exquisite curry tastes like it has been cooking all day, yet it can be ready and on the table in mere minutes. Serve it with basmati or jasmine rice, a cooling cucumber salad, and chapatis or whole wheat pita.

1. Heat the oil in a large skillet or Dutch oven. Add the onions and garlic, and sauté over medium-high heat until the onions are very tender and brown, about 15 minutes.

2. Reduce the heat to medium, and stir in the cumin, coriander, chili powder, turmeric, cinnamon, and pepper. Cook, stirring constantly, for 30 seconds.

3. Add the water, tomato paste, and sugar, and stir until well blended. Stir in the spinach and garbanzo beans. Cook, stirring almost constantly, until the spinach is wilted and the beans are heated through, about 5 minutes longer. Season with salt. Serve immediately.

1½ Tablespoons canola oil

1 cup chopped onions

1 teaspoon crushed garlic

2 teaspoons cumin

2 teaspoons coriander

2 teaspoons chili powder

1 teaspoon turmeric

1 teaspoon cinnamon

¼ to ½ teaspoon pepper

⅔ cup water

½ cup tomato paste

2 teaspoons sugar

4 to 6 cups coarsely torn fresh
    spinach, stems removed,
    lightly packed

3 cups cooked garbanzo
    beans, rinsed and drained

¼ teaspoon salt

Per serving: Calories 310,
Protein 12 g, Fat 8 g,
Carbohydrates 47 g

Fettuccine with Lemony Vegetables

Yield: 6 servings

Soothing noodles in a rich sour cream-style sauce form a sumptuous bed for crisp, tangy vegetables.

❧

3 cups silken tofu, crumbled

½ cup fresh lemon juice

¼ cup water

2 Tablespoons tahini

½ cup sliced scallions

½ teaspoon crushed garlic

1 pound fettuccine

1 to 2 Tablespoons extra-virgin olive oil

3 cups broccoli florets or asparagus spears, cut into bite-size pieces

2 medium zucchini, sliced thinly on the diagonal

1 Tablespoon lemon zest (see p. 139)

Lemon wedges

1. Combine the tofu, lemon juice, water, tahini, scallions, and garlic in a food processor or blender, and process into a smooth, creamy sauce. Set aside.

2. Cook the fettuccine in a large pot of salted water until tender. Drain well and return to the pot. Cover and set aside.

3. Heat the oil in a large skillet or wok, and stir-fry the broccoli or asparagus and zucchini until tender-crisp, about 8 to 10 minutes. Remove from the heat, add the lemon zest, and toss gently. Cover and set aside.

4. Pour the reserved sauce over the warm pasta, and toss well. Top each serving of pasta and sauce with a portion of the reserved vegetables. Garnish with lemon wedges, or pass them at the table.

Per serving: Calories 363,
Protein 18 g, Fat 11 g,
Carbohydrates 47 g

144

IGOR'S SPECIAL

Yield: 4 servings

*T*his quick pasta dish was contributed by my friend Paula Barry who prepares it often. Not only is it different and delicious, it can be on the table in a flash!

1. Cook the pasta in boiling water until just tender and before it has become al dente. Do not drain. Remove the saucepan from the heat and add the broccoli florets. Cover and let the pasta and broccoli sit for 5 to 8 minutes. Then drain the pasta and broccoli well in a colander.

2. Meanwhile, combine the tomatoes, onions or scallions, and walnuts in a large bowl. Add the remaining ingredients and toss to combine.

3. When the pasta and broccoli are ready, add them to the tomato and onion mixture and toss well. Adjust seasonings, if necessary. Serve at once.

12 to 16 ounces pasta (any kind)

4 cups bite-size broccoli florets

2 large, ripe tomatoes, chopped

½ cup chopped red onions or sliced scallions

½ cup coarsely chopped walnuts

2 Tablespoons fresh lemon juice

2 Tablespoons balsamic or wine vinegar

2 teaspoons extra-virgin olive oil

2 teaspoons organic flax oil

½ teaspoon crushed garlic

½ teaspoon curry powder

Dash *each*: pepper, cayenne pepper, salt, and natural soy sauce

Per serving: Calories 345, Protein 9 g, Fat 13 g, Carbohydrates 45 g

145

Fettuccine with Uncooked Tomatoes

Yield: 4 to 6 servings

*T*his dish makes a wonderful last-minute specialty. Fresh tomatoes and herbs contribute to its beauty and simplicity. Nothing could be lighter or easier for warm summer days when tomatoes and basil are abundant. Vegan parmesan cheese substitute, which is available in natural food stores, makes a terrific topping for this dish.

8 firm, ripe tomatoes, seeded and diced

½ cup chopped fresh basil

½ cup chopped fresh parsley

3 Tablespoons capers, drained (optional)

1 Tablespoon extra-virgin olive oil

1 Tablespoon organic flax oil

1 teaspoon crushed garlic

Salt and pepper

12 to 16 ounces fettuccine

1. Combine the tomatoes, basil, parsley, capers, oil, and garlic in a large bowl, and toss together gently. Season with salt and pepper.

2. Cook the pasta in a large pot of salted boiling water until tender. Drain well, and toss at once with the tomato mixture.

Per serving: Calories 328, Protein 13 g, Fat 8 g, Carbohydrates 50 g

Tip: *To seed a tomato, cut the tomato in half crosswise and gently squeeze out the seeds.*

146

Linguine with Spicy Red Garbanzo Sauce

Yield: 6 servings

A very satisfying entrée. For a cheesy-tasting finish, pass nutritional yeast flakes or vegan parmesan cheese substitute at the table. Because it makes a large quantity and doesn't require much attention while it cooks, this dish is great to prepare for company.

1. Combine the onion, water, celery, and garlic in a large saucepan or Dutch oven, and bring to a boil. Reduce the heat to medium-low, cover, and steam for 20 minutes. Remove from the heat.

2. Add the tomatoes, tomato paste, olive oil, dried herbs, salt, red pepper flakes, and pepper. Stir well until the tomato paste is evenly incorporated. Then add the garbanzo beans, and mix gently.

3. Bring to a boil. Reduce the heat to medium-low, cover, and simmer for 20 minutes, stirring occasionally. About 2 minutes before the end of the simmering time, stir in the fresh parsley.

4. While the sauce is simmering, cook the pasta in a large pot of salted boiling water until tender. Drain and return to the pot. Cover to keep warm, and set aside until the sauce is ready. Pour the hot sauce over the pasta and toss well.

2 cups chopped onions

1½ cups water

2 stalks celery, finely chopped

1 teaspoon crushed garlic

3 cups chopped canned tomatoes, drained

12 ounces tomato paste

2 Tablespoons extra-virgin olive oil

1 teaspoon *each*: oregano and basil

½ teaspoon *each*: salt and crushed red pepper flakes

¼ teaspoon pepper

2 cups cooked garbanzo beans, rinsed and drained

½ cup minced fresh parsley

16 ounces linguine

Tip: For smaller households, feel free to cut the recipe in half. It will work beautifully.

Per serving: Calories 333, Protein 11 g, Fat 6 g, Carbohydrates 57 g

QUINOA PRIMAVERA

Yield: 2 to 3 servings

Q uinoa cooks so quickly, this grain-based entrée can be on the table in under thirty minutes.

❧

1¼ cups water

½ cup quinoa, rinsed well

1 cup frozen green peas, thawed in hot water and drained

1 Tablespoon extra-virgin olive oil

1 medium carrot, thinly sliced on the diagonal

1 medium zucchini, thinly sliced on the diagonal

1 small red bell pepper, chopped

1 large leek, thinly sliced

½ teaspoon crushed garlic

1 teaspoon dill

Salt and pepper

1. Place the water in a medium saucepan and bring to a boil. Stir in the quinoa. Cover, reduce the heat to low, and simmer 15 to 18 minutes. Remove from the heat and scatter the peas on top of the grain; do not stir. Cover and let sit for 8 minutes.

2. Place the oil in a large skillet or wok, and heat over medium-high. Add the carrot, zucchini, red bell pepper, leek, and garlic. Stir-fry for about 8 minutes, or until the carrot is tender-crisp.

3. Add the quinoa, peas, and dill, and toss until thoroughly combined. Heat over medium-high, tossing constantly, until the peas are heated through, about 2 minutes. Season with salt and pepper. Serve hot.

Per serving: Calories 359,
Protein 14 g, Fat 8 g,
Carbohydrates 59 g

Bean & Bulgur Pilaf

Yield: 2 to 3 servings

This hearty pilaf makes a satisfying entrée. Just add a side of cooked greens to complete the meal.

1. Heat the oil in a medium saucepan. Add the tomato and sauté 4 to 5 minutes. Add the potato, beans, and stock or water. Bring to a boil. Stir in the bulgur and bell pepper. Reduce the heat, cover, and simmer until the water is absorbed and the potato is tender, about 20 minutes.

2. Season with salt and pepper. Serve at once.

1 Tablespoon extra-virgin olive oil

1 ripe tomato, peeled, seeded and chopped (see p. 137)

1 small potato, peeled and diced

1 cup cooked white beans or garbanzo beans, rinsed and drained

1 cup vegetable stock or water

½ cup bulgur

½ cup chopped bell pepper

Salt and pepper

Per serving: Calories 320, Protein 11 g, Fat 6 g, Carbohydrates 55 g

Baked Potatoes Florentine

Yield: 4 to 8 servings

*W**ith its luscious herb and spinach topping, this satisfying potato entrée will undoubtedly make you forget about dairy sour cream forever.*

4 hot baked potatoes (see Tip below)

1½ cups silken tofu, crumbled

⅓ cup minced fresh parsley

1 tablespoon extra-virgin olive oil

1 Tablespoon organic flax oil or additional olive oil

1 teaspoon *each*: dill and tarragon

½ teaspoon crushed garlic

Salt and pepper

10-ounce package frozen, chopped spinach

½ cup sliced water chestnuts, quartered (optional)

¼ cup thinly sliced scallions

Paprika

1. Combine the tofu, parsley, oil, herbs, garlic, salt, and pepper in a food processor fitted with a metal blade, and blend until smooth and creamy. Transfer to a medium bowl.

2. Cook the spinach according to the package directions. Drain in a wire mesh strainer or colander, pressing firmly with a fork or the back of a spoon to extract as much liquid as possible. Stir into the tofu mixture along with the water chestnuts, if using, and scallions. Adjust salt and pepper seasonings, if necessary.

3. Split the hot baked potatoes in half, fluff the flesh gently with a fork, and spoon the spinach mixture on top. Garnish with a light dusting of paprika.

Per serving: Calories 201, Protein 5 g, Fat 6 g, Carbohydrates 31 g

Tip: *To bake potatoes, first scrub them well. Preheat the oven to 375°F. Place potatoes directly on the center rack of the oven, and bake for 1 to 1½ hours, or until soft when gently squeezed. (Use an oven mitt!)*

Portobello Mushroom Steaks

Yield: 4 servings

These large meaty mushrooms make an exquisite entrée, especially when surrounded by brightly colored vegetables, such as green and yellow squash and cherry tomatoes. The beefy-tasting sauce mingles with the mushroom juices to create a rich, flavorful gravy. You won't believe how scrumptious, chewy, simple, and satisfying plant-based "steaks" can be! (These are pictured on the front cover.)

1. Combine the ketchup, vinegar, and garlic, and set aside.
2. Carefully remove the stems of the mushrooms, but leave the caps whole. Rinse the caps under water, gently rubbing with the surface of your thumb to remove any dirt.
3. Place a thin layer of extra-virgin olive oil in a large skillet, and heat over medium-high. If you do not have a skillet large enough to comfortably hold all 4 mushrooms at once, cook them in 2 batches or use 2 skillets. Place the mushrooms in the skillet, stem-side up. Cover and cook about 5 minutes.
4. Turn over and baste with the reserved sauce. Reduce the heat to medium. Cover and continue to cook until fork-tender in the center, about 5 minutes longer.
5. Season with salt and pepper. Garnish with fresh herbs, if desired. Serve whole or sliced on the bias (with the knife held at an angle).

¼ cup ketchup

2 Tablespoons balsamic vinegar

½ teaspoon crushed garlic

4 medium portobello mushrooms

Salt and pepper

Minced fresh parsley, chives, or scallions (optional)

Per serving: Calories 21, Protein 3 g, Fat 0 g, Carbohydrates 7 g

151

Mahvelous Millet Loaf

Yield: 8 servings

Millet is a highly digestible and versatile grain. Although it can be prepared fluffy and pilaf-like, it becomes soft and tender with a texture similar to polenta when it is cooked with a little extra water, making it an excellent foundation for a meatless loaf.

1 cup millet

2½ cups water

1 cup finely chopped onions

1 cup finely chopped or shredded carrots

1 cup finely diced celery

1¼ teaspoons salt

½ teaspoon crushed garlic

½ teaspoon thyme

2 Tablespoons extra-virgin olive oil

½ cup chopped pistachios

Pressure cooker method: Oil a large loaf pan or mist it with nonstick cooking spray. Set aside.

2. Rinse the millet well and place it in a 4½-quart or larger pressure cooker along with the water, onions, carrots, celery, salt, garlic, and thyme. Bring to a boil. Lock the lid in place, and bring up to high pressure over high heat. Reduce the heat just enough to maintain high pressure, and cook for 12 minutes. Remove from the heat, and allow the pressure to come down naturally for 10 minutes to complete the cooking process. Quick release any remaining pressure, and unlock the lid.

3. Stir in the oil and nuts, and mix well. Spoon the mixture into the prepared loaf pan, packing it down firmly. Place on a cooling rack, and allow the loaf to sit in the pan at room temperature for 15 to 20 minutes. Carefully turn the loaf out of the pan onto a cutting board or serving platter. Cut into slices and serve.

Per serving: Calories 249,
Protein 6 g, Fat 9 g,
Carbohydrates 35 g

Standard stovetop method: Oil a large loaf pan or mist it with nonstick cooking spray. Set aside.

2. Rinse the millet well and place it in a large saucepan along with the water, onions, carrots, celery, salt, garlic, and thyme. Bring to a boil. Reduce the heat, cover, and simmer for 30 minutes. Remove from the heat and let sit 10 minutes.

3. Stir in the oil and nuts, and mix well. Spoon the mixture into the prepared loaf pan, packing it down firmly. Place on a cooling rack, and allow the loaf to sit in the pan at room temperature for 15 to 20 minutes. Carefully turn the loaf out of the pan onto a cutting board or serving platter. Cut into slices and serve.

Artichoke Orgy!

I attended my first "artichoke orgy" well over twenty-five years ago. What a magnificent and memorable feast it was! My husband and I have faithfully carried on the tradition, and are delighted to share it with you here. Eating an artichoke can be absolutely sensuous—it's a wonderful experience to indulge in alone, with loved ones, or friends. Artichokes are a true delicacy and low in fat, with a flavor similar to the finest asparagus. When served with hearty whole grain bread or rolls, perhaps a salad or light soup for a starter, and a luscious dipping sauce, artichokes are an entrée in a class by themselves. Here's all you need to plan an artichoke orgy of your own.

Dipping sauce suggestions:

Low-fat or fat-free bottled salad dressing or salsa

Roasted Red Pepper Sauce, p. 126, or Classic Ranch Dressing, p. 73

Low-Fat Egg-Free Mayonnaise, p. 128, or your favorite low-fat vegan mayonnaise, about ⅓ cup per person (Thin it with a little plain nondairy milk, if necessary.)

1. Purchase beautiful looking, medium-sized globe artichokes. Wash them and cut off most of the stem, leaving about an inch or so. With a sharp knife, slice off the top of each artichoke about 1 inch down. With kitchen shears or scissors, snip off the sharp, barbed leaf tips.

2. Cook in a large pot of boiling water, covered, for approximately 35 to 45 minutes, or until a bottom leaf pulls outs easily. Invert in a colander to drain.

3. Cool. Then place in a covered container, and chill in the refrigerator until serving time. If you prefer, the artichokes may also be served warm.

Per artichoke: Calories 53, Protein 2 g, Fat 0 g, Carbohydrates 11 g

How to eat an artichoke: Place an artichoke on each dinner plate along with a small dish of the sauce to dip the artichoke leaves into. If you wish, have a separate large bowl in which to deposit the inedible parts of the leaves.

2. Start with the bottom row of leaves nearest the stalk. Pull off one leaf at a time, and dip the part that was attached to the artichoke into the sauce.

3. Place that part between your teeth with the inner part of the leaf facing downward towards your tongue, or upwards towards the roof of your mouth (whichever is your preferred style).

4. Draw the leaf between your teeth, pulling off all the tender, edible flesh. Discard the rest of the leaf. As you work your way towards the center of the artichoke, more of each leaf will be edible.

5. When you reach the fuzzy choke in the middle, scrape off the stringy, hard, or prickly parts and discard them. With a teaspoon, scoop out the center fuzzy portion of the choke. The part remaining is called the heart. It is entirely edible and is the meatiest, most delectable part of the artichoke. Cut it into pieces, dip it into the sauce, and savor every bite.

Tips: *To keep artichokes from discoloring, rub trimmed areas with lemon juice, or add a little lemon juice to the cooking water and put the artichokes in it as soon as they are trimmed. If desired, fresh lemon slices, garlic, or herbs may be added to the cooking water for extra flavor.*

Season the mayonnaise to your liking with one or more of the following:

- **Dry or prepared mustard**
- **Natural soy sauce**
- **Bottled hot sauce or cayenne pepper**
- **Fresh lemon or lime juice**
- **Crushed garlic or garlic powder**
- **Sliced scallions**
- **Minced shallots**
- **Grated fresh onion or onion powder**
- **Minced fresh herbs or dried herbs**
- **Curry powder, chili powder, or other seasoning blends**

ZUCCHINI RAMEKINS

Yield: 4 ramekins

A ramekin is essentially a rich, creamy, cheese-based pastry. The term also refers to the individual casserole dishes in which it is cooked. These particular ramekins are dairy-free, beautiful to behold, and scrumptious to eat.

❦

1 pound firm, regular tofu, rinsed, patted dry, and mashed

6 slices whole grain bread (crusts removed), crumbled

2 Tablespoons tahini

2 Tablespoons fresh lemon juice

¾ teaspoon salt

½ teaspoon *each*: basil, oregano, and thyme

Pepper

1 Tablespoon extra-virgin olive oil

2 cups diced zucchini

1 cup chopped onions

1 teaspoon crushed garlic

2 ripe tomatoes, sliced

About 3 Tablespoons nutritional yeast flakes

1. Preheat the oven to 375°F. Lightly oil four 15-ounce or 16-ounce individual casserole dishes, or mist them with nonstick cooking spray.

2. Place the tofu, bread, tahini, lemon juice, salt, herbs, and pepper in a large mixing bowl, and mash them together well using your hands to make a stiff dough. Set aside.

3. Heat the oil in a large skillet. Add the zucchini, onions, and garlic, and sauté until the onion is tender, about 10 minutes.

4. Fold the cooked vegetables into the reserved tofu mixture, and mix gently until well combined. Pack firmly into the prepared casserole dishes.

5. Bake uncovered for 15 minutes. Remove from the oven and place the tomato slices on top. Sprinkle with the nutritional yeast flakes, using about 2 rounded teaspoons per ramekin, and return to the oven to continue baking for 5 minutes longer. Let sit 5 minutes before serving.

Per serving: Calories 249, Protein 13 g, Fat 10 g, Carbohydrates 24 g

Tip: To safeguard your dinnerware, put a thick, folded cloth or napkin on each serving plate, and place the hot casserole dish on top.

⊕

CHAPTER X

SWEETS & TREATS

Aromatic Tea Cake

Yield: 9 servings

*F*ragrant with spice, this unusual cake has a sweet bottom crust and a moist, somewhat custardy top.

❧

2 cups whole wheat pastry
   flour

1 cup sugar

2 teaspoons cinnamon

½ teaspoon nutmeg

Tiny pinch of allspice

½ cup canola oil

1 teaspoon baking soda

1 Tablespoon flaxseeds

¼ cup water

1 cup silken tofu, crumbled

2 Tablespoons fresh lemon
   juice

½ cup chopped walnuts

1. Preheat the oven to 350°F. Lightly oil an 8 x 8-inch baking pan, or mist it with nonstick cooking spray.

2. Combine the flour, sugar, cinnamon, nutmeg, and allspice in a large bowl. Cut in the oil with a pastry blender or fork until crumbly and evenly distributed. Pat half this mixture evenly on the bottom of the prepared pan to make a crust. Stir the baking soda into the remainder, and set aside.

3. Place the flaxseeds in a dry blender, and grind into a powder. Add the water and blend until a gummy mixture is achieved, about 30 seconds. Add the tofu and lemon juice, and process until well blended. Pour into the reserved flour mixture, and stir until smooth and well blended. Stir in the walnuts.

4. Spoon the batter evenly over the crust. Bake for 30 minutes. Serve warm or cool. Cool completely before storing in an airtight container in the refrigerator for future use.

Per serving: Calories 338,
Protein 6 g, Fat 16 g,
Carbohydrates 40 g

APPLE CRISP

Yield: 6 to 8 servings

*S*weet apples blanketed with a chewy, granola-style topping are always enticing whether served for breakfast or dessert.

1. Preheat the oven to 350°F. Oil an 8 x 8-inch baking pan or 10-inch pie plate, or mist it with non-stick cooking spray. Set aside.

2. For the topping, combine the oats, flour, sugar, and nutmeg in a large bowl. Whisk together the juice concentrate and oil. Pour into the oat and flour mixture, and stir until crumbly and the oats are evenly moistened. Set aside.

3. For the filling, place the apple slices in a medium bowl. In a separate small bowl, combine the sugar, flour, and cinnamon. Sprinkle over the fruit and toss until evenly coated, making sure none of the mixture remains in the bottom of the bowl.

4. Arrange the fruit evenly in the prepared baking dish. Crumble the reserved topping evenly over it. Bake for 30 minutes or until the top is golden brown and the apples are fork-tender. Serve hot, warm, room temperature, or chilled.

Topping:

2 cups old-fashioned rolled oats

½ cup whole wheat pastry flour

¼ cup sugar

¼ teaspoon nutmeg

½ cup frozen apple juice concentrate, thawed

2 Tablespoons canola oil

Filling:

6 to 8 large Granny Smith apples, peeled and sliced

¼ cup sugar

2 Tablespoons whole wheat pastry flour

½ teaspoon cinnamon

Variation: *For* **Peach Crisp**, *substitute 6 to 8 large fresh peaches, peeled and sliced, for the apples.*

Per serving: Calories 342,
Protein 6 g, Fat 6 g,
Carbohydrates 66 g

DATE CAKE

Yield: 6 to 8 servings

*T*ake a cake on a date? No way! Feed cake to your date? Sure! Especially this
one, which is tender, moist, and power packed with wholesome whole grain
flour and flaxseeds, and sweetened only with pure, nutritious dates and fruit juice.
It makes a great morning coffee cake as well as a scrumptious snack cake or dessert.

❦

**2 Tablespoons ground
flaxseeds (see Tips at right)**

6 Tablespoons water

1 cup chopped dates

¾ cup water

**½ cup fruit juice (such as
apple, orange, or raspberry)**

¼ cup canola oil

**1½ cups whole wheat pastry
flour**

1 Tablespoon cinnamon

2 teaspoons baking powder

1 teaspoon baking soda

½ teaspoon nutmeg

1. Preheat the oven to 350°F. Lightly oil an 8 x 8-inch
baking pan, or mist it with nonstick cooking
spray.

2. Place the ground flaxseeds in a small bowl. Add
the water while beating vigorously with a fork.
Let sit until thickened and a little gooey, about 5
minutes.

3. Place the chopped dates and water in a blender,
and process until smooth. The mixture will be
very thick. Add the flax mixture, juice, and oil,
and process until well combined.

4. Combine the flour, cinnamon, baking powder,
baking soda, and nutmeg in a large bowl. Pour in
the blended mixture, and mix thoroughly. The
batter will be fairly stiff.

Per serving: Calories 247,
Protein 4 g, Fat 9 g,
Carbohydrates 37 g

160

5. Spoon or pour into the prepared baking pan. Bake until the edges of the cake begin to pull away from the sides of the pan and a toothpick inserted into the center of the cake comes out clean, about 35 to 40 minutes. Cool completely before serving. Store leftovers in an airtight container in the refrigerator for future use.

Tips: To make ground flaxseeds, place whole flaxseeds in a dry blender and process into a powder. Measure after grinding. Store any leftover ground flaxseeds in a tightly sealed container in the freezer, and use within a month.

*Variation: For **Almond Date Cake**, scatter ¼ cup thinly sliced or slivered almonds over the top of the cake before baking.*

This cake is highly adaptable. If you like, ½ cup chopped walnuts or ½ cup raisins can be folded into the batter after mixing. The cake is also attractive with a light dusting of confectioners' sugar sifted on top. Applesauce, fresh fruit, or berries would make a delicious accompaniment.

LEMON-APRICOT THUMBPRINT COOKIES

Yield: 2 dozen

These elegant cookies make a lovely gift, tea time snack, or company dessert. Oat flour is available in natural food stores. It can also be made at home by whirling rolled oats in a dry blender until ground into a powder.

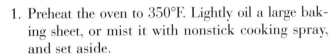

1½ cups whole wheat pastry flour

1¼ cups oat flour

½ teaspoon double-acting, non-aluminum baking powder (such as Rumford)

¼ teaspoon salt

½ cup pure maple syrup

¼ cup fresh lemon juice

¼ cup canola oil

Approximately 8 teaspoons fruit-sweetened apricot jam

1. Preheat the oven to 350°F. Lightly oil a large baking sheet, or mist it with nonstick cooking spray, and set aside.

2. Combine the flours, baking powder, and salt in a medium bowl. Combine the maple syrup, lemon juice, and oil in a separate bowl, and mix well. Pour this liquid mixture into the dry ingredients, and mix thoroughly. The dough should be stiff. If it is too soft to roll into balls, add a little more of either flour.

3. Using your hands, form into 24 walnut-size balls, and place on the prepared baking sheet about 1 inch apart. Make an indentation in the center of each ball with your thumb, pressing down lightly. Bake for 14 to 18 minutes or until lightly browned on the bottom.

4. Transfer the cookies to a cooling rack, and fill the cavities with a rounded ¼ teaspoon of apricot jam while the cookies are still hot. Cool completely before storing.

Tips: *If your thumb sticks to the dough when you are making the impressions, moisten it with a little water. Raspberry, blackberry, or strawberry jam may be substituted for the apricot jam, if you prefer.*

Per serving: Calories 86, Protein 2 g, Fat 2 g, Carbohydrates 13 g

Pumpkin Custard

Yield: 6 servings

*E*njoy *your favorite holidays and impress your guests with this delectable egg-
and dairy-free baked custard. It has all the goodness of pumpkin pie without
the hassle and mess of a high-fat crust.*

1. Preheat the oven to 350°F. Lightly oil 6 custard cups, or mist them with nonstick cooking spray.

2. Place the flaxseeds in a dry blender, and grind into a powder. Add the water and blend until a gummy mixture is achieved, about 30 seconds. Add the tofu, sugar, cinnamon, salt, ginger, and allspice, and process until well blended.

3. Pour the blended mixture into a bowl, and vigorously whisk in the pumpkin until smooth and creamy. Spoon into the prepared custard cups. Fill a large baking pan (large enough to hold all of the custard cups) with about one inch of water. Place the custard cups in the pan, and bake on the center rack of the oven until the custard begins to pull away from the sides of the custard cups and a toothpick inserted in the center comes out clean, about 50 minutes. Chill thoroughly before serving.

1 Tablespoon flaxseeds

¼ cup water

1½ cups silken tofu, crumbled

¾ cup sugar

1 teaspoon cinnamon

½ teaspoon salt

¼ teaspoon ginger

⅛ teaspoon allspice

1½ cups unsweetened canned pumpkin

Per serving: Calories 157,
Protein 4 g, Fat 3 g,
Carbohydrates 29 g

163

The Ultimate Chocolate Pudding

Yield: 1½ cups (3 to 4 servings)

*T*he name says it all. If you like chocolate pudding, this recipe is certain to make
you smile.

❧

1½ cups silken tofu,
crumbled

⅓ cup sugar or pure maple
syrup

¼ cup unsweetened cocoa
powder

1½ teaspoons vanilla extract

Tiny pinch of salt

Place all the ingredients in a blender or a food
processor fitted with a metal blade, and process until
smooth, creamy, and thick. Chill until ready to
serve.

Per serving: Calories 146,
Protein 6 g, Fat 4 g,
Carbohydrates 22 g

Rice n' Raisin Puddin'

Yield: 4 servings

*A*rborio rice is a short-grain Italian rice with a high starch content. It is traditionally used for making risotto because its starch gives this classic dish its requisite creaminess. For the same reason, arborio rice is ideal for making a lusciously creamy, but very low-fat, rice pudding.

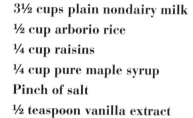

1. Combine the milk, rice, raisins, maple syrup, and salt in a medium saucepan. Bring to a boil, reduce the heat, and simmer gently, uncovered, stirring often, until the rice is tender and the liquid is thickened and creamy, about 45 minutes.

2. Remove from the heat and stir in the vanilla. Spoon into custard cups or a large serving bowl; cool. Serve warm or thoroughly chilled. Garnish each serving with a sprinkle of cinnamon, if desired. To store leftovers, cool completely, cover tightly, and chill in the refrigerator.

3½ cups plain nondairy milk
½ cup arborio rice
¼ cup raisins
¼ cup pure maple syrup
Pinch of salt
½ teaspoon vanilla extract
Cinnamon (optional)

Tips: *Do not rinse arborio rice before using. Rinsing will wash away the starch that contributes to its characteristic creaminess.*

The pudding will continue to thicken as it cools. For an even creamier pudding, increase the milk to 4 cups and extend the cooking time to 1 hour.

Variation: *For* **Fancy Rice Puddin'**, *add 1 bay leaf, ¼ teaspoon cardamom, and a good pinch of saffron to the mixture before cooking. Remove the bay leaf before serving. Omit the vanilla extract and cinnamon.*

Per serving: Calories 215,
Protein 7 g, Fat 4 g,
Carbohydrates 38 g

CRÈME ANGLAISE

Yield: 1 cup (2 to 4 servings)

*C*rème Anglaise is the French term for a rich custard sauce, commonly served over cake or fruit. In this dairy-free version, the fat content has been reduced to practically zilch, yet the opulent flavor is truly exquisite. As an added bonus, this recipe is unbelievably simple and readily adaptable. You can easily double it for larger portions or to serve more people.

1 cup silken tofu, crumbled

2 Tablespoons pure maple syrup

2 teaspoons canola oil

1 teaspoon vanilla extract

Pinch of nutmeg

Combine all the ingredients in a blender or a food processor, and process several minutes until very smooth and creamy. Serve at once, or transfer to a covered storage container and chill in the refrigerator.

*Variations: For **Fruit With Crème Anglaise**, stir ¼ to ½ cup of chopped fresh fruit or fresh berries into the custard.*

*For **Fruit Parfaits**, layer the custard with sliced fresh peaches and/or fresh blueberries or strawberries in small parfait glasses or wine glasses. Top the custard with an attractive arrangement of the fresh fruit, along with a fresh mint leaf, if available.*

*For **French Parfaits**, swirl 2 to 4 tablespoons fruit-sweetened preserves into the custard. Spoon the custard into small parfait glasses or wine glasses.*

Per serving: Calories 102,
Protein 4 g, Fat 5 g,
Carbohydrates 10 g

Mail Order Sources

Diamond Organics
P.O. Box 2159
Freedom, CA 95019
Phone: 800-922-2396
Fax: 800-290-3683
Organic fresh fruits and vegetables shipped direct.
www.diamondorganics.com

Gold Mine Natural Food Co.
7805 Arjons Drive
San Diego, CA 92126
Phone: 800-475-FOOD (3663)
Fax: 858-695-0811
A large selection of organic beans and grains, macrobiotic foods, and cooking equipment including pressure cookers.
www.goldminenaturalfood.com

Mail Order Catalog for Healthy Eating
P.O. Box 180
Summertown, TN 38483
Phone: 800-695-2241
Fax: 931-964-2291
Textured soy protein, seitan mixes, silken tofu, organic flaxseed, dairy-free parmesan, and nutritional yeast. Also vegan and vegetarian cookbooks.
www.healthy-eating.com

The New Mountain Ark
799 Old Leicester Highway
Asheville, NC 28806
Phone: 800-643-8909
Carries a wide variety of macrobiotic and vegan foods, grains, beans, nuts, dried foods, and cooking equipment.

Endnotes

1. American Heart Association, *1998 Heart and Stroke Statistical Update*, Dallas, TX (1997).

2. G. S. Berenson et al., for the Bogalusa Heart Study, "Association between Multiple Cardiovascular Risk Factors and Atherosclerosis in Children and Young Adults," *New England Journal of Medicine* 338:1650-6 (1998).

3. D. Ornish et al., "Can Lifestyle Changes Reverse Coronary Heart Disease?" *Lancet* 336:129-33 (1990).

4. J.W. Anderson and B.M. Johnstone, "Meta-analysis of the effects of soy protein intake on serum lipids," *New England Journal of Medicine* 333:276-82 (1995).

5. S.R. Gore et al., "Soluble Fiber and Serum Lipids: A Literature Review," *Journal of American Dietetic Association* 94:425-36 (1994).

6. A. Ascherio et al., "Dietary Iron Intake and Risk of Coronary Disease Among Men," *Circulation* 89:969-74 (1994).

7. American Heart Association, *1998 Heart and Stroke Statistical Update*, Dallas, TX (1997).

8. Margo Wooton, *Nutrition Action HealthLetter*, Center for Science in the Public Interest, January/February 1998.

168